THE TIMES OF INDIA

THE BEST OF
SPEAKING
TREE

VOLUME 7

Selections from 2011

A Times Group Presentation in Association with

THE BEST OF SPEAKING TREE - Volume 7

First published in August, 2012
First reprtint October, 2012

by
Bennett, Coleman & Co. Ltd.
7, Bahadur Shah Zafar Marg
New Delhi-110002

Acknowledgements
We thank all those who have contributed to "The Speaking Tree" column in
The Times of India during 2011.

Edit, Design, Marketed and Distributed by

Times Group Books
(A division of Bennett, Coleman and Company Limited)
Times Annexe, 9-10, Bahadur Shah Zafar Marg, New Delhi-110002

ISBN 978 93-80942-99-5

Printed at: Brijbasi Art Press Ltd.

Price: ₹250

PREFACE

or a mainstream newspaper which reports events from around the world, minus a great amount of tampering or analysis, The Times of India has been responsible in its mission. For more than a century and a half now, the daily has covered glorious highs as well as pitiful lows. Yet, for a long time there was no sense of a deep-seated satisfaction that came from a job well done.

It was this sense of dissatisfaction, disenchantment and a drive to move beyond mere reporting (mostly of brutalities, death and destruction) that gave rise to The Speaking Tree. This column has been a forum for readers to decipher, understand and accept disturbing events/news in a philosophical way. At a very basic level, it helps readers to cope in an all-too-familiar context the relevance of religion, spirituality and philosophy. At a higher and far more sublime level, these columns assist readers to sift the transient from the permanent, the truth from the web of deception and wisdom from a maze of unfurling lies. It aspires to provide hope and comfort to fatigued minds, turbulent hearts and burdened spirits, and provides security in the knowledge that ultimately it is this hope and the strength derived from it that keeps the human spirit afloat.

The present volume consists of the more stimulating presentations of the column. Every contribution, needless to say, is potent enough to transform human abilities, capabilities and his interface with life and its ebbs. We offer this book to you with the great hope that it will open up your mind and soul, inspire your spirits and become a sweet companion along the walk of your life.

Indu Jain
New Delhi, August 2012

CONTENTS

CONTENTS

CONTENTS

Introduction

he popularity of the previous volumes of 'The Speaking Tree' has prompted us to come out with yet another. Like the pieces in the previous volumes, those here will help the reader in understanding the complexities of human existence, in picking their way through the maze of confusion and in charting for themselves a path which promises peace and happiness.

This book is in fact a wholesome mix of food for thought. If you treat it as a book of spiritual recipe and follow the instructions laid down therein, you stand to reap endless benefits as you discover new avenues of peace, joy and fulfilment, resulting not from pleasures of the senses but from spiritual awakening, from discernment of right and wrong and from attainment of wisdom.

Like the earlier volumes, this one too is full of nuggets of wisdom gained from self-realization, deep thought processes and first hand experiences. Every aspect of life is viewed from a new angle. Here are a few samples:

Love tainted with selfishness is 'attachment'. Get attached to a wider circle of people — community, nation, humanity. As you get attached to the higher you get detached from the lower.

Look at others as part of yourself and you will focus on their best qualities. You will see opponents as partners, competitors as comrades. You will celebrate their victories as if it were your own.

Material prosperity tends to erode character, value and behaviour in some. This is something that we need to guard against. Test of our behaviour is not how we treat VIPs or those who matter to us but how we treat people who are less fortunate than us.

Grief and delusion come as a result of identification with body, mind and intellect — the little self. The moment you look at things from a personal angle there is sorrow. View the same thing from a larger perspective and peace prevails.

When a person carries baggage more than his capacity to carry weight, his face becomes distorted in pain. Similar is the case when one's personality carries the heavy load of ego and self-interest.

This book is replete with such words of practical wisdom. Delve into it, absorb what you read, practise it and evolve into a better soul.

Of Ends & Beginnings

Marguerite Theophil

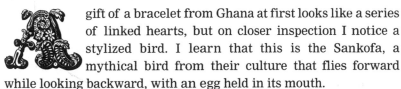 gift of a bracelet from Ghana at first looks like a series of linked hearts, but on closer inspection I notice a stylized bird. I learn that this is the Sankofa, a mythical bird from their culture that flies forward while looking backward, with an egg held in its mouth.

The word Sankofa derives from the Akan people, a West African ethnic group that today resides in Ghana and the Ivory Coast. The Akan, over centuries, developed a highly artistic and communicative system of ideographic and pictographic symbols, each representing a specific concept, proverb or saying rooted in the Akan experience. These symbols can be found used extensively in indigenous textiles, metal and wood work, jewellery and architecture, too.

The older African religions had no sacred texts. Their beliefs were handed down mostly orally through proverbs and stories or through pictorial symbols that convey the deeper meanings of life and culture to a community or nation. A proverb from which the concept and meaning of Sankofa is derived declares, "It is not wrong to go back for that which you have forgotten." It speaks of taking from the past what is good and bringing it into the present in order to make positive progress through the benevolent use of knowledge.

The Sankofa bird is stylized in a circular fashion to represent that there is no end and no beginning. It has an egg in its mouth, which represents not only the knowledge of the past upon which wisdom is based, but also signifies the generation to come that would benefit from that wisdom. Culturally, the Sankofa bird represents the collective wisdom of a people, and teaches that a people must know its legacy to understand their present situation in order to protect and create a future for generations to come. It is a message to take from the past what is good and bring it into the present in order to move forward with a strong foundation. It can also remind us that we are all here because of the sacrifices of those who have gone before. Another translation of this concept is "You can't know where you're going unless you know where you come from," and this can hold for individuals as much as it can hold for cultures. I see this in practice when as individuals we look at the things that happened in our past, take what we have learned from those experiences, and use it to move forward, and when this helps us also to avoid creating the same unhelpful patterns again and again.

Sankofa represents the concepts of claiming identity, redefinition, revisioning and acting — which are key aspects of personal growth and work. It reminds one to focus on moving forward, while gaining wisdom from the past and achieving proper balance in preparation for the future. Many of us bury in the past not only problems, but also often the best and most valuable parts of ourselves. Sankofa is a wonderful teaching here, reminding us that in such cases, 'returning and fetching that which is lost' is not at all wrong, and often necessary. Whatever we have lost, forgotten, given up or been stripped of, can be reclaimed and revived. We are encouraged to reach back and gather the best of what our past has to teach us, reclaim the lost or marginalized aspects of our higher selves, so that we can achieve our full potential as we move forward.

Gita & Business Ethics

Arun K Gupta

usiness ethics is the code of good conduct that a business adheres to in its daily dealings both with other businesses and with customers. Most philosophers conclude that ethical failure occurs because of lack of character. Virtuous people will live ethically. Therefore, we need to think about the desired virtues and how one can develop those virtues.

In the month of Magha (December) 5,000 years ago, on the battlefield at Kurukshetra just before the start of Mahabharata war, Krishna outlined to Arjuna a system of ethics that has withstood the test of time. In the *Bhagavad Gita*, Krishna tells Arjuna not only how to build character but also the root cause of ethical failure and how to avoid it.

Krishna outlines 26 qualities of a gentleman — to be merciful, obedient, truthful, equitable, saintly, magnanimous, mild-mannered, clean, simple, charitable and peaceful. He should have surrendered to God and not be greedy or possessive but remain steady and determined, free of the six bad qualities, not gluttonous, sober, respectful, humble, grave, compassionate, friendly, eloquent, expert and concise.

It is easy to give a list of positive qualities that we can all agree upon. Yet, even though hundreds of trainers work day and night to teach people good character, when it really matters, people's character still fails. Why?

Krishna answers in chapter three, verses 37 and 38: "O Arjuna, it is lust... later transformed into wrath, which is the all-devouring sinful enemy of this world. As fire is covered by smoke, as a mirror is covered by dust, or as the embryo is covered by the womb, the living entity is similarly covered by different degrees of this lust."

To maintain good character, we must overcome *kama*, that is, lust or selfish desire. Most people think *kama* means just sexual craving, but it simply refers to an overwhelming desire for anything, such as lust for power. Greed, dishonesty and corruption are all byproducts of lust. To be happy, successful and well-situated, the *Gita* says, one must control lust.

Gita's solution to the ethical failure and downfall of corporations and society and family is controlling the senses with spiritual strength. Ethics is linked to spirituality. For the last century or more, western businesses separated work and spirituality. Kurukshetra was also about mind control. Every one of us, whether as manager or employee, is fighting his own battle, his own Kurukshetra. The *Gita* can help us to learn to regulate our senses, control our minds and gain spiritual strength.

The *Gita* is as fresh in insight and as relevant today as it was 5,000 years ago. If only every manager, administrator, politician, employee, worker and others pick a copy of the *Gita* and spend a few minutes daily reflecting on its message, one can experience the positive transformation. Who doesn't wish to be disciplined, to achieve home-work balance and bring peace and harmony in a secular environment?

Experience Life's Rhythm

Purnima

Hoysala king who was on a hunting expedition captured a gorgeous white baby elephant that got separated from its mother. The elephants of noble breed belonged to the king of the neighbouring region. But gradually the baby elephant was turning out to be naughty and ill-mannered. The king who was concerned about its impudence with the mahout, handed his minister the responsibility of tracing the cause. The minister hoisted himself on a tree close to the baby elephant to keep a watch on him through the night. As night approached, he saw some men of ill-repute sitting near the baby elephant. They were badmouthing people, exuding anger and vengeance. This went on for several days. The minister duly reported this to the king who had the men barred from that place. He now sent a group of wise people to keep the baby elephant company. Very soon, the baby returned to its natural state of goodness and virtuosity.

Can we hope to always be surrounded by good people or be in a good environment? Life is unstable and unpredictable. How can we insulate ourselves from the bad effects? The solution is to have a 'living mind', a mind that is watchful and observant. When the mind is dominated by suspicion, anger, fear, hurt or anxiety, it becomes dead and fossilized. It loses its ability to enquire into anything, be it an event or an emotion. It becomes compulsive, mechanical and repetitive. Such a mind devoid of awareness and alertness is prone to fall a victim to the vagaries of the world. It is weak and helpless. A mind that is awake and watchful nurtures goodness, virtue, joy and love within a human being in all aspects of life. A dead mind can only brag about its ideals of goodness and integrity but in reality its actions are prompted by fear, confusion and rigidity. It is fossilized thinking. Awareness is what can give you an extraordinary quality of life.

There are different views about life. Some say it is predestined; others say it is an accident and that it has no destiny. But there is a

17

destiny and it is crafted by our thoughts. This is how we create our destiny:

- Thoughts
- Moods
- Actions
- Emotions
- Temperaments
- Destiny

When we do not throw the light of awareness onto our thoughts regarding a particular situation, it precipitates emotions like anger, hurt and fear. When these emotions are not attended to, we get used to them and they cause mood swings. Thereafter, it becomes our second nature, our temperament. Just as layer upon layer of sedimentation solidifies into rock, continuous unawareness and ignorance go to make our personality. We become defined, limited and controlled by them. Our actions would then be directed by our moods. Such unintelligent action would lead to a poor destiny, devoid of love, joy, abundance or success.

Hence, 'a living mind' which is vigilant about what it thinks and feels is of utmost importance to create a great destiny. Destiny is also not created in one moment; it takes shape with each situation life throws up and with each response you give to it. So come alive, live consciously, be aware of every movement, and be awake to every rhythm of life. In living life every moment that you see is each time a new beginning.

Body, Mind & Spirit

Shri Shri Anandamurti

uman existence is trifarious, a combination of three currents: physical, mental and spiritual. Most people may not transcend the limits of their physical existence: they get enmeshed in crude worldly pleasures, tormented by desire. Subtleties of life, expression and practice are perhaps beyond their reach. Their world is limited to their bodies and physical requirements. There are others who are more concerned with their minds as they feel that it is the supremacy of mind that sets them apart. Their lives are guided by their desires for mental satisfaction.

By virtue of their endeavours they create poetry, art, music and sculpture, for instance. They express the finer human feelings of mercy, sympathy, love, friendship and pity. They believe that the mind flows for the sole purpose of attaining the Infinite, and hence they focus their energies on the contemplation of the Transcendental Entity. They are spiritual aspirants. Drawn by the magnetic attraction of Cosmic Consciousness they speed forward and reach the stage which marks the end of mental existence and the beginning of spirituality.

At that stage one is no longer a human being, one is a veritable god. It ought to be the mission of every person to achieve confluence of the mental and spiritual strata. It is the pinnacle of human progress. It is the beginning of divine existence. The meeting point of the highest attainment of humanity and the blossoming of divinity is the base on which the cardinal human principles are established. Looking back, it is evident that nowhere have human values been truly honoured. What is worse, nobody has looked upon humanity with sympathy.

Only those were respected who, by serving their self-interests, climbed onto the higher rostrum of society. It is difficult to step down from the high position of the vainglorious to rub shoulders with the less privileged. The neglect of humanity was particularly acute towards the end of each era of the social cycle. The progeny of the noble *kshatriyas,* the physically strong, on gaining power, engaged themselves in the pursuit of pleasure and comforts, utterly neglecting their sacred duty to serve their people.

They never cared to know people's suffering. Kind-hearted and philanthropic kings did exist, but very few, if any, met the psycho-physical needs of his people and opened the gateway to realization of the Infinite. For self-aggrandizement and in a bid to conquer the world they invaded countries, one after another. How could they afford to inquire into the tragic plight of the common people? The *Vipra* era or intellectual era illustrated the same thing: the scholarly *Vipras* were hardly accessible to the common people.

The innocents were busy appeasing the *Vipras* with oblations, honorariums and floral offerings. Service to the needy might not yield immediate results but the potential for future benefit is immense. Rabindranath says, "By standing aloof from your fellow man daily, you have hated the God enthroned in his heart." Instead of hating anyone, the *Sadvipras* — physically fit, mentally strong and spiritually elevated — will encourage everyone to build good careers. This will be *Sadvipra's* principle duty. None should feel that they have been doomed forever.

True Beauty of Being

Jug Suraiya

n Galsworthy's *Forsyte Saga*, Soames, the rich and acquisitive Man of Property, is enthralled by the beautiful Irene. He wants to possess her beauty, the way he possesses the grand mansion he buys for her, full of exquisite and expensive works of art. But the harder Soames tries to claim her as his own, the more he repels Irene. The only man she is comfortable with is the elderly Jolyon. While conscious of her beauty, the ageing Jolyon has no desire to possess it. In the twilight of his life, he basks in her radiance as a man warming himself in front of the glowing embers of a fire on a cold day.

Soames and Jolyon represent two very different perceptions, not only of beauty but of consciousness itself. Like most of us, Soames wants to lay claim to the beautiful — which is another word for perfection — and make it his own. In his case, the beautiful, or the perfect, is represented by a woman.

In the case of a poet or an artist, the beautiful could be represented by the music of language or the splendour of a sunrise which the creative imagination seeks to capture in a line of verse or by brush strokes on canvas.

But beauty can't be owned by an individual: the poet and the artist know that what they create is of value only if it belongs to the whole world and not to themselves alone. Unlike Soames, the Man of Property, Jolyon, like the poet and artist, understands that beauty can never be a possession; it is always and essentially a celebration, a glimpse of perfection all the more haunting in its elusiveness.

As William Blake said,
"He who bends to himself a joy
Does the winged life destroy;
But he who kisses the joy as it flies
Lives in eternity's sunrise."

Soames wants to possess Irene's beauty, and is doomed to fail; Jolyon celebrates her beauty and is rewarded by the glow of her

21

presence. These two ways of perceiving beauty belong to two distinct categories of consciousness: being and having. Being is consciousness without the attached strings of attachment and ego. Being is a way of seeing the world, and everything in it, through the consciousness of a poet, or an artist, or a sage. Being has no title deed, no desire of possession, no stamp of ownership.

The polar opposite of being is consciousness in the mode of having. The world and everything in it — beauty, wealth, power and fame — is perceived as possession, something to have and to hold on to at all cost.

If being is pure consciousness without ego, having is pure ego without consciousness. In having, the ego becomes all-consuming: my wishes and desires that must be fulfilled, my ideal home, my perfect family, my enviable collection of art and beauty, my good name and reputation, the world as my private property to do with as I will.

Without Irene and her unattainable beauty which he covets to keep for himself, the Man of Property becomes a spiritual vacuum. Without the desire to have and to possess, Soames's counterpart, Jolyon, is enriched beyond measure by Irene's beauty. Jolyon has discovered the beauty of being.

The Secret of Parenting

Swami Sukhabodhananda

he beautiful atmosphere of the *ashram* encompasses the serenity around it. It is very pleasant to be in the *ashram*. One mother experiences unpleasantness all around her. The serene atmosphere of the *ashram* makes no difference to her. She shares her concerns for the upbringing of her children in this world. How was she to keep them away from drugs, alcohol and glamour? She cries with fear and pain, "Swamiji, my life is miserable whenever I think of my children in this wicked world. What should be my approach to the bringing up of my children?" Often I question the very genesis of such an enquiry.

When we operate out of fear, we transmit the energy of fear to our children; in a subtle way, of course. If we were to operate out of trust, we would transmit trust to our children. We have to realize that our actions are born from our thoughts. Our thoughts are the products of our values, we get what we focus on; so focus that good things would happen to our children. This is one of the strong variables, which would impact our children. But the mother asks lovingly, "Why do children detest advice?" The question is, are they really against advice or the way we administer it? Every parent should be sensitive to this aspect.

Children are not against advice; but they are very sensitive to the way it is administered. The heart of education is the education of the heart. "How can I learn to advice in this manner?" asks the mother. Have you observed birds building nests? They build in such a way that when it rains, not a drop of water falls in the nest. How did the mother bird learn the art of such an engineering feat? It is said that when the mother bird is pregnant, intuitively this knowledge arises. Love for the offspring brings out this latent wisdom to build the nest.

Let your love guide you and not fear. Love will show you the way. The mother nods in affirmation that love is the supreme power. A boy complained to his grandmother, "No one likes me at school and

23

life is bitter. My teachers reprimand me, friends are better than me in sports, some friends are better than me in studies and I feel bitter about life."

"Shall I make a cake for you?" asked the grandmother.

"Good, I badly need to sweeten my life," said the boy.

After some time, she gave him flour. "This is not cake, it is so bitter," screamed the boy.

Then she gave him little baking powder. Again the boy screamed, "This is not cake, it is so bitter." Then she gave him an egg.

"This is not cake, it is not tasty," screamed the boy. Then the grandmother lovingly told the boy, "Individually each one of them is not tasty but when put together; it becomes a cake. In the same way," she said, "individually your experiences are bitter; but join them together with commitment and transformation. Add the sugar of your being and make it a cake. Life is like cooking, you should just make it."

What is the yoga of wisdom? It is that power of love is God and love for power is ego. What is yoga of action? It is that love recognizes opportunities and does not wait for its introduction.

We Create Our Life

Osho

lways wait for something good and it happens, because whatsoever happens, we create. In fact, we create it; we sow the seeds. But we sow the seeds unconsciously, that's why we think that some accident has happened. Accidents never happen, nothing is ever accidental. It is a cosmos, it is not a chaos.

Everything is absolutely based on a fundamental ultimate law: nothing ever goes wrong. Yes, sometimes it looks to us as if it has gone wrong, because we were expecting something else. That's a problem — we do one thing, we sow one seed and we expect something else. We sow the seeds of one kind of flower and we expect some other kind of flower, so when the flowers come we are frustrated. But flowers come through the seeds, not our wishes.

So remember: We constantly create our world. There are people who are constantly afraid that something wrong is going to happen, and then it happens! And when it happens, they are proved right. They have made it happen... People who are afraid will always find situations in which fear grips them. People who are loving will always find situations where love blooms. Because this existence goes on giving you that which you project.

Life is our project. We are our life's creators. God has created man, but as freedom. So there is an essential freedom inside; now it is up to you to choose what you would like to happen to you in life and then you will see that it starts happening. One thing is linked with another, one thing leads to another, and slowly you have taken a certain route; then all other alternatives are dropped.

When a child is born, all the alternatives are open; he is utterly free. He can be a musician, poet, wrestler, a politician, he can be anything... an Adolf Hitler, a Gautama Buddha; anything is possible. But sooner or later choices start coming and he starts moving in a certain direction. Then that direction remains his world. So always remember: whatsoever has happened to you, you have been the cause of it. Sometimes it hurts that you are the cause of all the misery that has happened to you; you feel sad. But there is no need to feel sad, because through it, you come to an understanding, and then things need not happen the same way again to you.

And the second thing to remember is: For every hurt or happiness always feel thankful, because sometimes pain is needed for growth and pleasure is not needed. So whatsoever happens, make it an opportunity to grow. Use that opportunity as a springboard for something higher. A friend dies, there is pain, there is anguish and misery, but use that opportunity. Meditate on death. Your friend's death has reminded you of a very significant phenomenon that death is there.

Don't arrange your life without taking note of death. Maybe existence has given you a message to get ready: the friend is gone, you will be gone one day, so prepare for death! Life is a small affair; a 70-year affair in which one-third will be gone in sleep, another one-third will be gone in earning bread and butter, another one-third in other stupidities... Nothing much is left! It is not a big thing, it is a very small phenomenon; compared to death it is nothing. Death is eternity.

New Life for Vivekananda

Deepak Chopra

ew Life for Vivekananda? It's time. Ever since I was young there has been a halo around the name of Swami Vivekananda, as there was around his master's, Sri Ramakrishna. Recognition outside India meant a lot a hundred years ago; it was an enviable kind of validation. But to be candid, none of this reverence affected my life. Vedanta was just an arcane term, and the flight of modern Indians was toward science, upward social mobility and personal freedom. I imagine that anyone who took the step of joining the Indian diaspora followed the same wave that carried me to America.

It was years before I realized what I'd run away from, and now Vedanta means a lot to me. It is the map to higher consciousness, never surpassed by later history yet frequently validated in fresh, new ways Vivekananda did that a century ago. We honour his memory for it, but that's incidental, for the spiritual path implies action, not salute to memory Vedanta is either here and now or it is nowhere. Which means that without new life Vivekananda's legacy will be inert. The only viable memorial is to put his model of spirituallty into practice.

I'm avoiding the phrase 'put his ideas into practice', because Vedanta, once reduced to ideas, is equally lifeless. So what would Vivekananda ask us to do today, here and now? First, to put into practice his famous adage: Jiva is Shiva. A lifetime can be richly devoted simply to these three words. They tell us that individual God-realization is possible; also that external deities exist only to point inward. Further, they imply that inner transcendence is the path to reach the Absolute. None of this is news, and it would be easy to gather countless aspirants who strive to put these words into practice in their daily lives.

What is the secret of success, since so many of these aspirants fall short of the goal? The secret is: There is no goal. The present moment is the home of Vedanta and also the home of Self-realization. The present moment isn't heading anywhere; it has no goal or end-point. Seen as Vivekananda would see it, the now is eternal; it is the only time that renews itself endlessly. In the now we experience two things only: the rush of events, both physical and mental, and the background of consciousness which acts like the screen upon which experience is registered.

Experience is passing scenery; consciousness is silent observer. For most, these two are jumbled together. Caught in the rush of experience, they've lost the silent observer and so cannot walk through the door that opens to the transcendent. Vivekananda's work was mainly occupied with revealing the transcendent. He left many inspiring reminders to point us in the right direction: "You have to grow from the inside out. None can teach you, none can make you spiritual. There is no other teacher but your own soul. You cannot believe in God until you believe in yourself." And, "The goal of mankind is knowledge. No knowledge comes from outside: it is all inside." Reminders in this case are actually goads to action. The first duty of every person is to develop a true self. This cannot be done without the inner knowing that Vivekananda embodied as did Vedic sages. The time is always right for transcendence. No worldly accomplishments are substitutes nor as worthy as the project of developing a true self. The best way to honour Vivekananda begins at this very moment, with each of us.

Of Ego & Will

Pandit Rajmani Tigunait

any people believe they need a strong ego to live a successful life and to progress in their spiritual pursuits. This is not true. We cannot be successful in either the external or internal world while we are tossed about by a powerful ego. What success in both realms does require is a strong will. The difference between ego and will is that the ego is blind but the will has vision. Will has its source in the pure Self. Ego springs from *avidya,* a false sense of identification with the external world, and is usually concerned with preserving self-image and self-identity.

Ego is characterized by stubbornness, selfishness, and unwillingness to compromise. The ego is like a little pool. An egotistical person is like a frog crouching in that pool — his world is small, his borders insecure. He has only a vague awareness of the trees around the pool, and he cannot begin to imagine the frog-filled marshes just beyond. From his perspective, only his own feelings and his own voice are meaningful. The power of will, by contrast, is like a spring whose source is the Pure Being. It infuses the mind and body with enthusiasm, courage, curiosity, and the energy to act.

This intrinsic power of the soul is called *iccha shakti,* and it is from this force that all the various aspects of our personality, including the ego, derive energy to carry out their activities. Becoming successful in the world requires a strong will, and that strong will needs to be properly guided so that we develop a strong personality rather than a trivial, egotistical one. A strong personality exhibits tolerance and endurance. It has the power to 'vanquish' an opponent, but chooses to forgive and forget instead.

When egotistical, on the other hand, we demonstrate our weakness by answering a pebble with a cannon. We lose composure the moment our feelings are even slightly bruised. We have a hard time forgetting injuries we have received from others, but an even harder time remembering how much we have injured others. All the problems in the world — at home, at work, in politics, everywhere — are caused by colliding egos. These problems are not overcome by one ego dominating others, but by a person of strong will and clear vision coming forward and overshadowing the trivial egos of those who are quarreling.

A strong ego is as much of an obstacle in spiritual practice as it is in worldly matters. The stronger the ego, the bigger the hurdle it will create. However, the solution is not to kill or weaken the ego but to do our best to purify, transform, and guide it properly. We can do this by employing both our intelligence and our power of discrimination. In other words, when we meditate, practice contemplation, pray, study the scriptures, serve others, and seek the company of the wise we make our ego purer and less confined, and this in turn inspires us to move one step forward.

As we do, the purified ego, accompanied by a sharpened intellect, gets a glimpse of the next level of awareness, and naturally aspires to reach it. Thus the ego becomes the tool for purifying and expanding itself, and in this way the petty ego is gradually transformed into an expanded, more purified ego. Along the way it becomes increasingly apparent that this transformation must end with the ego dissolving and becoming one with the pure Self and experiencing its union with Universal Consciousness. As the ego of a dedicated seeker merges with the Infinite, all confusion disappears, the veil of duality lifts, and the purified ego sees the whole universe in itself and itself in the whole universe.

Focus on Your Breath

Swami Kriyananda

oncentration is the key to success. The student taking an exam, but distracted by a popular song running through his head; the businessman trying to write an important contract, but worried over an argument that he had that morning with his wife; the judge, distracted by the fact that a teenager to whose defence he is trying to listen bears a striking resemblance to his own son: All of these persons could tell us something of the disadvantages of poor focus.

A focused mind succeeds not only because it can solve problems with greater dispatch, but also because problems have a way of somehow vanishing before its focused energies, without even requiring to be solved. A focused mind often attracts opportunities for success that, to less focused (and therefore less successful) individuals, appear to come by sheer luck.

Concentration awakens our powers and channels them, dissolving obstacles in our path, literally attracting opportunities, insights and inspirations. In many ways, subtle as well as obvious, concentration is the single most important key to success.

The mind, in meditation especially, must be so perfectly still that not a ripple of thought enters it. God cannot be perceived except in silence. Of these techniques, my guru, Paramhansa Yogananda, considered the most effective to be one which involves attentiveness to the natural process of breathing... The simplicity of this technique causes many a beginner to ignore it; yet in its very simplicity lies much of its greatness.

Concentration implies, first, an ability to release one's mental and emotional energies from all other interests and involvements, and second, an ability to focus them on a single object or state of awareness. Concentration could be dynamic outpouring of energy to perfectly quiescent perceptions and in its higher stages, it becomes so deep that it is no longer just practice: The yogi becomes so completely identified with the object of his concentration that he and it, as well as the act of concentration itself, become one.

In this way he can even, temporarily, become one with something external to himself, gaining thereby a far deeper understanding of it than would be possible by scientific objectivity. But focusing on our own higher realities, identification with them becomes lasting. For we are the infinite light, and love, and joy, and wisdom of God. Consciousness of diligent practice ought to be refined into an effortless process of divine becoming.

The most effective technique of concentration will be one which both interiorizes the mind, and permits a gradual transition from technical practice to utter stillness. The technique of watching the breath fulfils both of these requirements — better, perhaps, than any other technique possibly could. For not only is the breath one of the most natural focal points for attention, the more deeply one concentrates on it, the more refined it becomes, until breathing is automatically and effortlessly suspended in breathlessness: Meditator, the act of concentration, and the object of concentration, become one.

The Light of the Sun

Soma Chakravertty

ho has time nowadays for reflection? But it is only by devoting a bit of time to this activity can we explore awareness of being, oneness with universal spirit and celebration of a healthy and happy life. We need light to show us the way that can take us towards the higher Self. What could be a better path-shower than what is referred to as the 'Living God', the Sun? The sun is perceived as the co-creator and sustainer of life on earth. The sun's rays blend with our aura to enrich receptiveness of cosmic energy and guidance. This universal light force can be used in the ongoing process of cleaning, balancing, healing and evolving. This can create conditions that can enable us to be more positive, aware and sensitive and take initiative while driving away negative emotions.

What needs our attention most, according to Sri Surya Jowel (Sooryaji) is the effort to elevate our mind and transform our lifestyle. "For this we require a light and energy source that can reach the dark corners of our mind and reveal to us life in its true perspective. And what could be better than the living energy source of the entire solar system, the sun?" This cosmic energy imbibed through eyes at sunrise (*sooryayog*) can heal, elevate and transform us, which in turn can bring about shift in perception for a better world. We create our own surroundings.

Sunlight is nature's gift to mankind. We need the sun to survive and to be healthy in body and mind. The rays of the sun contain seven different colours which correspond to our energy centres or *chakras*. Unique vibration of each colour in the rays of the sun can be used as tools for healing physical, psychological and spiritual ills.

Each of these *chakras* is related to a basic element. The mooladhar (basic *chakra*), the earth element, is red. The swadesthan (sex) *chakra* is orange with water as its element, and fire is associated with the manipura, the solar plexus. The colour of anahat or heart *chakra* relating to air element, is blue, the visudhas or throat element is ether. The colour of the third eye or ajna *chakra*, the forehead, is indigo — the light element while sahasrar or crown *chakra*, violet, signifies pure awareness. Thus when we take in sunlight at dawn, these *chakras* or subtle energies help to balance and promote healing — physical, emotional and spiritual. The earth receives the highest degree of positive energy at sunrise. At that point of time the human organism is most receptive towards solar energies. In fact, an hour before sunrise, solar energies exert positive psychological influence on the cells of the body, as they refresh and invigorate them. The sun's rays improve digestion and enhance nutrition, quicken blood circulation, facilitate elimination of impurities through skin, and make bone structure stronger. Sunlight lifts one out of depression and thereby helps to elevate the mind.

Sun can bring about transformation in body, mind and spirit that well could be gradual but a fulfilling experience ultimately. "As within, so without" — Sooryayog is all about discovering Sakha, your Atma Soorya or the inner sun that could be your best friend.

Times are Changing

Henryk Skolimowski

e aspire to enlightenment and truth; we're convinced that genuine spirituality is an indispensable vehicle for our ultimate quests. We are less certain that traditional religions are necessary for our inner lives. And we are doubtful if science can play a major role in our ultimate fulfilment, especially as science has been tainted and is partly responsible for the world's pollution and our psyche.

Yet the allure of science is formidable and sometimes irresistible. Since Swami Vivekananda's participation at the Parliament of World Religions in Chicago in 1893, many attempts have been made to reconcile religion with science. They failed because of at least two reasons. One was that scientists and their institutions were never truly interested in such reconciliation. Believing that science is truth, scientists tend to look at spiritualists with condescension, if not contempt. Scientists implicitly demand that spirituality subsumes itself into the matrix of science and its truths; or better still that science is recognized as the supreme religion.

The second reason for the face-off is more fundamental. Spirituality and science dwell in two different universes. The former is governed by empirical truths, while the latter is governed by spiritual truths. Science is about measurable facts while spirituality is about immeasurable like love and bliss. But are facts always all that clearly defined?

Naked facts do not exist. Facts are fictions of our theories. Karl Popper has demonstrated this convincingly. Times are changing. Many have come to the conclusion that humanity in the future will develop outside the foundations of science and technology, but predominantly on spiritual foundations. In this context the bell is tolling for science. Science must work out its own spiritual foundations, yes, by going deeper into cosmic principles which underlie its existence, yes, by reading the laws of the universe with

35

a new depth and imagination. Science must base itself on cosmic and not empirical foundations alone, for, empirical foundations are so flimsy. I never speak about religious foundations or religious truths but only about spiritual ones.

We should be aware that the tables are now reversed. Science must have the humility to learn from the tradition of spiritual truths. I am not talking about religious dogmas. I am talking about the underlying matrix of spiritual truths, which pervade the cosmos — thus these principles and insights, which enabled the human mind to transform the mundane and the vulgar into the transcendent and divine, which enable us to overcome brutishness in favour of love, which enable us to share altruistically all the riches of this wonderful universe.

My discourse has relevance for the existing spiritual traditions. They also leave something to be desired. They are too partial, too self-centred, too isolated. They also need to look much deeper into the underlying structures and principles of the universe. The search for the source has not ended. The understanding how it is all connected in the underlying structure of harmony and beauty is still beyond our grasp. There are many partial truths. But great truths are not that many. Do we have courage and wisdom to rally around these great truths — with compassion and without competition?

In closing: the bell is tolling for science and for existing spiritual traditions. They both need a renewal at the fundamental level.

Love & Meditation

Prasanna Guru

I f some of us have felt the essence of love, the difficultly arises in keeping the flame of love alive. The very moment one transfers the experience of love into words and memory, the mind takes over, only to end up in creating an unreal picture of love.

It is imperative to understand the fact that love can be felt only in the present. And all thoughts of love deny love and push the individual to ignorance so that one is in the unreal world of love.

The individual gets mired in the web of thoughts which is basically of attachment and dependency. The built-up thoughts about love which bring false happiness, inexorably give way to pain and suffering arising out of losing it. Only an individual who is integrated, harmonious and sensitive can keep the flame of love going. It becomes indispensable for the individual to stay rooted in the present, so as to be in the pool of love. And only an individual who is in love with himself can know the art of loving others.

After knowing that love blossoms and expresses itself in the present moment, the question of whether one is rooted in the present becomes inevitable. If one is in the present and in love with himself and others, then meditation does not mean anything to him.

If you feel that you are not in peace, harmony and in exuberance, then meditation is a tool that can bring you back to love and life. Meditation creates the space in you so that you can witness your own insensitivity and habits. This very seeing of your own insensitiveness opens the doors of sensitivity in you.

This sensitivity of seeing one's own shortcoming triggers the channel of intelligence. Seeing yourself and others without the interruption and interpretation of the mind, frees the mind so as to be active and alert. The natural flow of moving along with the life source makes you supple and receptive. False images which were products of the mind break down in front of reality. As an individual you once again regain your original innocence of being with yourself and flowing with the present. This being in the present inexorably opens the doors of love which comes along with pure intelligence to face reality without remorse.

Meditation cleanses the dust of ignorance that accumulates over time. The more you use meditation to get back to your source, your inner Self, the more you become aware of your unconscious repressions which were hindering you from knowing your potential. Once the unconscious repressions are brought out and they pass through the channel of the conscious mind, you become free of bondages. Without this release, any attempt to love yourself and others becomes an exercise in futility.

Meditation bridges the conscious and unconscious, helping the individual to set himself free from his own bondage. And only the one who has freed himself from the fetters of mind can come back to his natural state — which is love itself. Only a loving person can be with reality and face it intelligently. Meditation becomes the tool which takes the individual to merge with the very ocean of love which is in one. Ultimately the individual comes to face the truth that meditation is in love personified.

Live a Life of Totality

Swami Sukhabodhananda

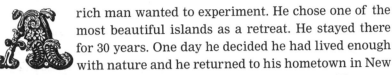

rich man wanted to experiment. He chose one of the most beautiful islands as a retreat. He stayed there for 30 years. One day he decided he had lived enough with nature and he returned to his hometown in New York City. He was asked many questions by journalists: "How was the island? What kind of experience did he have? Could he describe the changing seasons there; what kind of flora and fauna did he find there? Did he encounter wildlife? What made him stay so long there?" He heard all their queries patiently and at the end said, "My God, I did not know the island was so beautiful. If only I had known about its beauty earlier, I would have looked at each element more closely!"

Here was a man who lived on a beautiful island, and who was apparently oblivious to many of its unique features. Often we are like that. We do not observe things closely. And when we don't observe things closely, we start looking at things very superficially. That means living a life of deficiency, mired in *samsara*. To live life deeply is to live a life of inner freedom, of nirvana.

All enlightened masters, out of deep compassion, try to rouse humanity awake. They try to wake us up because we've been asleep too long. Imagine a multi-storey building. Suppose, you are living in the basement and you have not explored the other floors of the building. If you are only looking at the basement of the multi-storey building, your view of the world from the basement is going to be limited. If a consultant comes and says — you are living in a multi-storey building, why are you confined to the basement? How ridiculous and foolish it looks. If you are the owner of the multi-storey building, why don't you explore the rest of it and know it better and put it to good use?

I am saying this because throughout the verses of the Bhaja Govindam, Adi Shankaracharya says *"Mudhamate, mudhamate, mudhamate"* — Fool, fool, fool. He says this out of deep love as we are living a tepid life. We are not living a life of totality. As the Bhaja Govindam unfolds, he is inviting us to wake up to a higher dimension of living. When we open our eyes; our third eye, we see *Soundarya Lahari* — waves and waves of beauty. The whole text of Bhaja Govindam in essence means 'Wake up, seek the Lord, and stop seeking the crude, the superficial and the inessential things in life.' Therefore, the whole text of Bhaja Govindam has to be listened from a sincere heart.

These enlightened masters disturb our slumber but they don't put us to sleep. We are cozily asleep, lost in our belief and in our dogmas; they come and wake us up, shake us up and pull us out from our comfort zone, which is not really our comfort zone. It is only supporting our lethargy. Our comfort zone is not really allowing us to grow. It is protecting us and cementing our lethargy. Therefore, great saints' call is to wake us up. All words of enlightened masters are really an invitation to waking us up.

Thus, one has to listen to the words of Adi Shankaracharya from such perspective. I have always been emphasizing that when you listen, listen very carefully. More often people listen from different dimensions.

Love is in the Air

Sri Sri Ravi Shankar

f there is anything in this universe that cannot be defined, it is love. If you can describe love, then it is far from the truth. You give flowers, you hug, you prostrate, you offer but still something remains unexpressed.

Once Rama asked Hanuman: 'Tell me how much you love me?' Hanuman said, "My Lord, I cannot express my love for you, you want to see? I will tear open my heart and show you."

Even if for your whole life you try to express how deep your love is, you cannot express it fully. You can only find a little expression, just a glimpse of it.

There are three types of love: *satvik, rajsik* and *tamsik. Satvik* love is that which does not expect anything in return. *Rajsik* love is the love combined with feverishness and a desire to get something back. *Tamsik* love is just to destroy things. But Divine love is free from all these three.

Worldly love can be like an ocean, yet even an ocean has a bottom. Divine love is like the sky which is limitless, infinite. From the bottom of the ocean, soar into the vast sky. When you love somebody, what do you love in them? Do you love their qualities, attributes or the person? Often love diminishes. A child loves its mother and as the child gets older, the love for the mother recedes as the focus is now on friends, then spouse and then children. Divine love, however, grows every moment...

You can never be bored being with a wise person, a saint. Every day you spend, you feel the depth is getting even more. Every moment you spend with a saint you feel the relationship is growing deeper and deeper. This kind of love never breaks down; it never diminishes. Divine love is so refined and so subtle, it cannot be expressed; it can only be experienced.

Mysteries cannot be understood; they cannot be explained, but can be lived. *Sukshmataram Anubhavarupam*, it's a form of experience. You can live it, you can be it, you can shed tears of gratitude, but you

41

cannot express it. You cannot fully share it with anyone. This love is so unconditional; it does not depend on the behaviour of the other person. It does not depend on the attributes of the other person. And it does not depend upon what they do to you and what they don't do to you. You are in love because you can't be but in love. You have no choice as it is your very nature. Like the sun has no other choice than just shine. The sun is anyway shining beyond the clouds. Nothing can stop the sun from shining. Even when an eclipse happens, those shadows are so far away from the sun. It does not touch the sun. Similarly, all the seeming disturbances in love, in your life, do not take away your nature, which is pure love, unconditional love.

The ability to receive genuine love comes with the ability to give love. That's why often you do not know how to respond when someone shows a lot of love. The more you are centred and know by experience that you are in love, the more you feel at home with any amount of love expressed in any manner. Deep inside, you know that love is not an emotion; it is your very existence.

Unburden Yourself of Ego

Arup Mitra

hen a person carries baggage more than his capacity to carry weight, his face becomes distorted in pain. Similar is the case when one's personality carries the heavy load of ego and self-interest. A constant conflict, a feeling of perpetual dissatisfaction and irritation with the self and the rest of the world are some of the obvious outcomes. This creates a huge barrier between the person who carries the baggage and all others who are around him. He becomes unpopular, unpleasant and emotionally volatile.

We are aware of all this, yet we do not make efforts to reduce the weight of the baggage. The Sankhya system of Indian philosophy mentions the concept of *jivan-mukti*, that is, attainment of salvation while still alive. In this state of mind, there is freedom from bondage. The mind has to be free of ego and its natural instinct to pursue self-interest based activities. However, that state of thoughtlessness has to come spontaneously and through practice for which simplicity of mind is a prerequisite. The more selfish we are, higher is the probability that we become complicated, losing simplicity of mind.

Being materialistic, one loses the quality to appreciate, for example, the beauty of the dawn and to remain engrossed in it. If one cannot become engrossed, the state of thoughtlessness cannot prevail. The *Bhagavad Gita* suggests the path of complete surrender in order to get rid of ego. Ramakrishna realized how difficult it is to surrender ego since our way of life makes it an indispensable part of our existence. So he says if it has to stay, let it remain as a slave. I am here to serve the Almighty — in thinking this let that 'I' become subservient.

Tagore shows the path of taking pride in the love of God. Tagore glorifies 'self' in such a wider and greater context that it loses its independent existence and merges with the universal. Aggregation of individual maximization may not lead to social maximization always. If each one of us pursues self-interest there can be possibility of conflict as two objectives can be contradictory to each other, leading to violence. Yet, two opposite beliefs can continue to appear rational in their own places and rights and hence, it will be difficult to reject one of them on the ground of rationality.

However, selfless action — the capacity to think beyond 'I, me, myself' and to pursue action beyond those limits — can reduce substantially the possibility of such conflicting outcomes. Selfless action is, therefore, an important way of attaining salvation in life. Altruistic individuals in a society dominated by self-centred people can get exploited. But that does not mean one has to give up the altruistic attitude or the desire to pursue selfless action. Every time the sage picks up the scorpion from the water to save its life, it stings the sage. In the process his hands shake and the scorpion again falls into the water. But the sage does not stop there: he bends down again to pick it up from the water. When asked why he was doing this repeatedly, the sage replied he was only doing his dharma just as the scorpion was doing his. Only selfless action can deliver peace and bliss. Sharada Devi, therefore, suggested if we need peace in life let us not find fault with others; we need to identify our own pitfalls first. If we cut down on our heavy baggage of ego and self-interest a bit, it won't be difficult to realize the vastness within us and find joy in life.

The Satisfaction of Loss

Janki Santoke

The *Bhagavad Gita* talks of our capacity to take joy and loss equally. But we find happiness only in one, not the other. Profit, victory, success are pleasure. Loss, defeat, failure are not. Loss is deprivation. It is to be looked down on; to be avoided at all costs. It is a sign of failure. It is considered a tragedy. A sportsman losing his gold or a lover losing his beloved is used with great dramatic and emotional effect. Yet there is a satisfaction which can be experienced in loss. Melancholy is not altogether negative. It can be dignified and can demonstrate character. Wordsworth calls it 'majestic pain', such that the immortals feel... You might wonder, how can one experience satisfaction in loss? It seems counter-intuitive to think that in loss there can be peace. But there can be peace in loss. Because in that situation there exists something other than the result: it is the action. Deep satisfaction can arise from having done the best one could possibly do.

Swami Parthasarathy talks of the joy of action well-accomplished. To strive, to struggle, and to not succeed must be your motto, he says. This seems a bit strange. What use is struggle if it doesn't result in success? Results are not under our control. Just because you did your best doesn't mean you get the reward. There is no such law. If this is so, why would one work? Because, even though results are never guaranteed, satisfaction can be! You can be entirely content by doing your action perfectly. The pain of loss will be offset with the bliss of satisfaction with oneself. If you have left no stone unturned, done all you could possibly do and yet failed, there is still a great feeling of satisfaction within. The action itself brings satisfaction. There lies the importance of dedication in work. That you worked hard and gave what you could makes you strong enough to bear the loss, if any. The peace continues despite the loss. The pain will not be accompanied by sleepless nights. Sorrow will not give rise to agitation. That much can be guaranteed in a world of very few guarantees.

Satisfaction in loss can be experienced in yet another way. When one knows, finally, that nothing can be done, craving ends and you experience peace. The result has come in, the suspense is at an end and nothing remains to be done. You have done what you could. The mind is at rest.

This of course is not to be misconstrued as the martyrdom of self-pity usually demanding others' pity too! It is not about wearing one's heart on one's sleeve and using one's misfortunes as a talking point, or enjoying one's pain. It is not a game to be played to avoid effort. It is not complacency with the less-than perfect. It is simply finding happiness which is within our control instead of depending on factors over which we have no control. It is a peace that comes, spontaneously, out of a job well done.

There is tremendous power in action. "May you live a hundred years working," says the Isavasya Upanishad. Action brings about satisfaction, prosperity and purifies the personality. Then losses and gains become insignificant. And happiness becomes consistent. That's why it is said that to be a loser' is not all that terrible — in fact it could do you good.

Don't be in a Hurry

Maulana Wahiduddin Khan

man who was very fond of trees wanted to see a green tree in the courtyard of his home. He thought that if he planted a sapling, it would take a long time to grow into a tree. So he went to a garden and selected a fully grown tree. He then employed several labourers to dig it up and then transport it to his courtyard where he had it planted.

The man was very happy. He thought to himself: "I have travelled a long journey in a single day. Planting a sapling or a seed would have been a lengthy business and now I have found a quick way of having a lush green tree."

But the next morning when he looked at the tree, he found that its leaves had begun to wither, and after a few days the whole tree dried up. He was disappointed. When one of his friends visited him, he found him very sad. When he asked the reason, he said, "I am in a hurry, but God isn't."

This story instructs us about the law of nature, which is based on gradual development and not on sudden leaps. One who follows this law of nature will be successful, while the one who fails to follow it, will be doomed to failure. This law of nature is applicable not only to trees; it is a universal law. In every field, one must follow this natural course; otherwise one cannot attain any worthwhile goal.

Why is it that when the tree was in the garden, it was green, but when the same tree was transferred to another place — the courtyard — it dried up? The reason is that when the tree was in the garden, it had its roots intact, but when it was transferred to the courtyard, it had very few of its roots left. And it is roots that give life to a tree.

This is a law of nature and this law of nature applies to all human activities. It is the need of every business, every profession, and every institution to have proper roots, that is, a sound basis. There is no exception to this law of nature.

For example, education is the basis for a job, reputation is the basis of a business, and infrastructure is the basis of national development. Laying a solid foundation requires a long time; you cannot have such a foundation by just taking wild leaps. When you are in a hurry to achieve something, it means that you are denying the law of nature. You want to build a world on your own and this is not possible in this world. Those who engage in a gradual process will find support in nature; and without such support no achievement is possible.

Why did God decree this gradual process as the course of nature? He did so for the purpose of consolidation. If you try to achieve something by leaping into things, the final result will be like an uprooted tree. But when you adopt the gradual process, you consolidate your achievement.

An agriculturist once rightly pointed out that it requires only six months to grow a *kakdi* plant, but if you want to grow a tree like the oak, it will take 50 years to produce a fully grown tree. From this example one can understand how the law of nature functions.

The Gateway to Bliss

Jaya Row

editation is the highest spiritual technique that needs to be practised diligently and devotedly by qualified practitioners. The essential prerequisite is a calm mind. A mind burdened with desires and attachments is unable to take off into subtler realms of concentration and meditation. Entitled 'The Yoga of Meditation', chapter 6 of the *Bhagavad Gita* elucidates meditation as the final gateway to Self-realization.

Krishna begins with the definition of a *sannyasi*, a renounced person. Renunciation is not giving up enjoyments, abandoning one's duties and escaping to a safe sanctuary. It is this misunderstanding that has turned away genuine seekers and prevented them from accessing the benefits of renunciation. Krishna describes a *sannyasi* as one who does what one ought to do, fulfils one's duties and responsibilities fully, without depending on the fruit of action.

A *sannyasi* is not one without a higher ideal, nor is he an inactive person. Krishna describes the three stages of spiritual evolution, from an active yogi to a meditative *sannyasi* and, finally, to the exalted state of a *jnani*, the enlightened One.

A *sannyasi* has offloaded the bulk of his desires and is in contemplation of the higher. He is fit for meditation and embarks on the path of deep reflection and focus on reality. A *jnani* has reached the exalted state of enlightenment. Krishna describes the three stages in terms of mental states rather than external appearances.

Step by step, Krishna takes us through the preparatory disciplines as well as disqualifications for meditation. One must have a balanced contact with the world — neither too much nor too little. Every activity must be carefully supervised by the intellect so that no desire interrupts the subtle practice of meditation.

Krishna then gives the test of enlightenment. A realized soul is one who feels one with everyone. He sees his Self as the Self in all beings. In the end he worships God not in a temple, church or mosque, but in every living being. Thereafter, he lives in *atman*, whatever his lifestyle. It is pointless to declare love for God when you cannot connect with His images everywhere.

Arjuna, like us, is afraid of leaving the safe confines of his present existence to discover the unknown realm of the Infinite. He asks Krishna what the fate is of those who commit themselves to a spiritual life but die before realization. Krishna gives a fitting reply to reveal one of the most insightful laws of life. He says, "One who is righteous will never come to grief — either now or in the future." Your efforts will not go in vain. You will carry forward the credits to your future life.

A spiritually evolved person who falls short of realization will either be born in the home of the happy and wealthy or in a family of wise yogis. There, endowed with the wisdom acquired in previous lives, he will strive even more to attain enlightenment. Thus the diligent seeker effortlessly reaches Brahmn. The key words are vairagya, dispassion and *abhyasa,* practice. One must be convinced of the futility of worldly passions and pursue the necessary spiritual practices consistently.

In Love, Pain is a Blessing

Osho

ove is painful, but the pain is certainly a blessing. Love is painful because love brings growth. Love demands, transforms and is painful because love gives you a new birth. Love brings your heart into relationship — and when the heart is in relationship there is always pain. If you avoid the pain, you will miss all pleasures of life. With love you become human; you stand erect on earth. With love you are vertical. With love are problems. But with problems is growth — the greater the problem, the greater the opportunity for growth. More and more pain, too. That's why many people never love — it is so painful. They never become vertical.

Love never shatters you completely. It simply shatters you a little, a little bit. It shatters the crust of your ego, but the centre of the ego remains intact. Then there is a deeper pain, deeper than love, and that is of prayer — it shatters you utterly. It is death. When you have learnt how to love, and you have learnt that the pain that love brings is a blessing in disguise, it is beautiful, then you become able and you take another step — that step is prayer.

All lovers feel a little miserable. They would like to disappear completely, but it is not possible in human relationships. Human relationship is limited. But one learns from it, that there is a possibility: if it can happen so much in a human relationship, how much more can happen in a relationship with the Divine?

Love makes you ready to take the final jump, the quantum leap. That's what I call prayer, or you can call it meditation. You have to disappear for existence to be. Love is a training ground, a school, to learn first lessons — of the beauty, of the blessing and benediction of disappearance; to learn that pain is blessed. So when you are in love, or when love arises, cooperate with it, don't try resisting. People come to a compromise. The basic problem that I have been looking at is that lovers by and by come to a compromise. The compromise is: You don't hurt me, I will not hurt you. That's what marriage is. Then people become settled. They become so afraid of pain that they say, "Don't hurt me and I will not hurt you." But then when pain disappears, love also disappears. They exist together.

When you are in love, love hurts. It hurts terribly. But never resist, never create any barrier for pain. Allow it. And by and by you will see that it was a wrong interpretation. It is not really pain. It is just that something is going so deep in you that you interpret it like a pain. You don't know anything else. You are only aware of pain in your past life, in your past experience. Whenever something penetrates deep, you interpret it as pain. Don't use the word 'pain'. When love and love's arrow goes deep into your heart, close your eyes and don't use words — just see what it is, and you will never see it is as pain. You will see it is a benediction. You will be tremendously moved by it. You will feel joyous. Don't use words. When something new happens to you, always allow a deep look into it without any language.

Mind, Body & Self

Prabhakar V Begde

here are three aspects to an individual. His persona as people think he is, as he himself thinks he is, and what he actually is. People judge you mostly by your outward manifestation in terms of your personality, attire, the way you carry yourself and your status in society. You judge yourself by what you think you are capable of doing, while others judge you by what you have already done. An individual's perception about himself is mostly coloured by the twin conditions of self-importance and ego, albeit in varying degrees. Very few are keen to find out the real Self hidden within to ascertain one's true identity. Knowledge of the Self is one of the most important fundamentals of philosophy.

The Brihadaranyaka Upanishad states, "Whosoever departs from this world without having realized his own inner world, to him, life has been of no service. It remains unlived, like unrecited Vedas or any other undone deed."

"It seems to me ridiculous," said Socrates, "when I am not able to know myself, to investigate irrelevant things." Augustine puts across the importance of Self-realization a bit differently in his *Confessions* to convey the same meaning, "Men travel to gaze upon mountain heights and the waves of the sea, broad-flowing rivers and the expanse of the ocean, and pass by themselves."

In Self-awareness there is immense joy. The Self is *chetana*, supra-consciousness, the knowledge of pure existence. All the pain and misery is a result of not knowing the Self. The divine in us manifests itself only when we subject ourselves to certain disciplines. The divine operates in us, but it requires an effort to make it shine forth. The epistemological corollary is that man gets knowledge by looking inward, either at his own consciousness or at the revelations it receives from another superior consciousness.

What is the difference between man and animal? When we look at animals, with their perceptual and instinctive consciousness, we observe the inadequacy of the principle of life. As life outreaches

53

matter, so does the mind outreach life. There are forms of life without consciousness but there can be no consciousness without life. The mind in an animal is of a rudimentary character. As humans, we have the play of intelligence. Intelligence frames concepts and ideals, plans means for realization.

Conditioning of the mind is the most important theme of Indian philosophy and the first step towards Self-realization.

The body is called *kshetra*, the field, and within it dwells the owner of the body and the Supreme Lord, who knows both the body and the owner of the body. Perfect knowledge of the constitution of the body, construction of individual soul, and the constitution of the Super-soul is known as *jnana*. To understand both the soul and the Super-soul as one, yet as being distinct, is knowledge. According to the *Bhagavad Gita,* one who studies the subject matter of the field of activity as well as the knower of the field can attain knowledge.

The prayer of every heart is outlined in the Brihadaranyaka Upanishad thus:

"*Asato maa sadgamaya,*
tamaso maa jyotirgamaya,
mrityorma amritamgamaya."
— "Lead me from the unreal to the real,
Lead me from darkness to the light,
Lead me from death to immortality."

Up Your Self-esteem

Janina Gomes

n important lesson in life is to value ourselves. If we do, we will walk with confidence and see ourselves and our experiences from the right perspective. We cannot avoid people holding us and our achievements in contempt. Once we learn to believe in ourselves, our innate goodness and our value as unique beings created in God's image and likeness, we will start living from a different paradigm. We will also begin looking at others as fellow human beings, all on the path to the divine and sharers in this journey of life.

All areas in life are important — looking after ourselves and maintaining ourselves physically, keeping our spirits high and in tune with the divine, widening our horizons, keeping ourselves centred and being conscious of the spiritual and divine. Innate value is something that is independent of the circumstances of our birth, socio-economic status and the slot we occupy in life. We will find that all the joys of sharing a simple life and a humble position have led us to add value in life. Values are often equated with moral values. While the most fundamental moral values are almost universal, life does not stop with morality. Life is also about giving and taking, about love and friendship, about generosity and vision.

We will find that even if unconsciously, we all have a mission statement in our lives. This mission statement will encompass all the good we do in life and all the potential we develop to do good to others. On the other hand, if we continue with narrow motives, what we would have, really, is a distorted view of the world. With narrow world views we will judge others by our own subjective standards that are coloured often by prejudice and acrimony. If, on the contrary, we look at life as an open book on which we write messages of harmony, brotherhood and sisterhood; encourage others to brave living and see our actions as a furtherance of the divine purpose, our lives will be informed by the values that are close to true humanity. True humanity is represented by true values. We will not look only for gains but for opportunities to serve others. Everything in nature has an intrinsic value — fields, flowers, trees, sky, infinite space, stars and all living beings. As human beings, we need to realize our true potential and value.

Once we realize our intrinsic value, we will stop playing to the gallery, we will not look for constant approval or appreciation. Whatever we do, we will rest in the assurance that we have contributed something worthwhile. This means that we accept ourselves as we are and remain content with what we have so far achieved. We do not respond to put-downs or rejection with despondency or a sense of failure. We do not miss the point, even if others have about us. It is strange how we sometimes have to experience 'failure' many times before something 'works out'.

Trial and experimentation are part of the process. We become more giving in our relationships, and receive life with open hands. Yes, it is possible, in fact probable that people will devalue us. But once we know who we are — precious children of a common God who is Father to all — we will value ourselves and our lives as a gift from God. Whatever we do, say or become — we will become worthy children of God. "Not a sparrow falls from the skies without His knowledge."

Towards Harmony of Faiths

Balmiki Prasad Singh

arendra Dutt, better known as Vivekananda, established the Ramakrishna Order to share and spread the values of Vedanta, and reach quality education and healthcare to as many people as possible. Swami Vivekananda renewed people's interest in religion. He promoted inter-faith harmony. Hence his teachings are of great relevance, particularly in the current context. For Vivekananda, service to God meant service to the disadvantaged. He coined a new word, Daridra Narayana — seeing God in the less privileged — and it was upheld as a religious axiom.

Like the Buddha, Vivekananda promoted rationality in human conduct so that religion relates to intellectual conscience and rational thinking. That way, it would appeal to a wider audience. Any religion that divides people or exalts privileges, encourages exploitation and instigates wars cannot be justified. Hence his was a gender-neutral espousal of lofty religious values that he believed would help expand human consciousness. According to Vivekananda, we need to renounce hatred and cultivate love and compassion for all; only then can we begin to live in peace and harmony.

It is not possible to live an isolated life. As more and more people migrate to urban areas, an increasingly greater number of people of different faiths live side by side. Hence there is the need for greater understanding of each other's aspirations, faiths and beliefs as well as practices. To Vivekananda, Vedanta was not Brahmanism or Buddhist, Christian or Muslim. Vedanta was the sum total of all of these. In his historic address to the Parliament of Religions in Chicago on September 11, 1893, Swami Vivekananda clarified as follows: "The Christian is not to become a Hindu or Buddhist, or a Hindu or a Buddhist to become Christian; each must assimilate the spirit of the other and yet preserve individuality and grow accordingly." Ramakrishna Paramahansa said, "As many opinions, that many ways." Swamiji greatly valued plurality of approach in human affairs and spoke against uniformity that ends any kind of diversity.

Vivekananda said: "The greatest misfortune would be if all were to recognise and accept but one religion, one universal form of worship, one standard of morality. This would be the death-blow to all religious and spiritual progress." The Ramakrishna Order takes care of each and every member's food, clothing, shelter and healthcare needs. It motivates its personnel through rigorous training and idealism.

Terrorists are using religious slogans to justify their gross deeds. But how could a man of religion be a terrorist? How could a religious person join a suicide squad if he believes in service of the disadvantaged? Swamiji's answer was to encourage plurality of faiths and harmony among religions. Swami Vivekananda declared in the Parliament of Religions that "If anybody dreams of the exclusive survival of his own religion and the destruction of others, I pity him, and point out to him that upon the banner of every religion will soon be written, in spite of resistance: 'Help and not Fight', 'Assimilation and not Destruction', 'Harmony and Peace and not Dissension." As we celebrate the 150th birth anniversary of Swami Vivekananda, let's also celebrate all that the young monk stood for.

Lowest Form of Giving

Oswald Pereira

Dear Bill Gates and Warren Buffett,

Each time you visit India and open a window to your fortune for philanthropic causes here, smiles light up the faces of those who might benefit from your generosity. Then as soon as you've gone, the joy you brought them goes, too. Why, despite the generosity of "financial saints" like you, you end up leaving a charity-sized void in the lives of those you set out to uplift? Why are they not content? Are they not satisfied with your generous aid?

Mother Teresa figured it out in a way when she said, "There are many in the world who are dying for a piece of bread, but there are many more dying for a little love." But then love, too, soon turns out hollow, unless sustained by something more substantial, like commitment. You have both committed a great deal of your wealth to help those in need of material help. Isn't your philanthropic legacy, the greatest act of love and commitment to date?

I'm not so sure. For, to sustain love and commitment, one needs to share knowledge. And knowledge-sharing is not all about imparting education as we understand it to mean. Perhaps the answer lies in the *Bhagavad Gita*. In Chapter 4, Krishna talks about transcendental knowledge and says that material giving should be transcended by a higher form of giving. Krishna tells Arjuna: "O chastiser of the enemy, the sacrifice performed in knowledge is better than the mere sacrifice of material possessions. After all, all sacrifices of work culminate in transcendental knowledge" (4:33).

The *Gita* makes material *yagya* or sacrifice the lowest form of giving. Vedic scriptures do talk of meritorious rewards one reaps with ritualistic sacrifices, rigorous asceticism or by philanthropic charity. However, the one perfected in the science of uniting individual consciousness with Ultimate Consciousness transcends them all and achieves the supreme, primordial abode (8:28).

The *Gita* devotes an entire chapter to Karma Yoga, the path of action. As you mature on this path, you continue to perform good deeds — philanthropy may be one of them — but with less doership. Charity can be transformed to a spiritual plane only if it leads to reduction of one's ego and doership; doing good with perfection but without attachment.

The Bible puts charity on a high spiritual plane. "And though I have the gift of prophecy, and understand all mysteries, and all knowledge; and though I have all faith, so that I could remove mountains, and have not charity, I am nothing" (1 Corinthians 13:2). However, in most versions of the Bible, the word charity is substituted with the word "love". It seems then that the Bible elevates charity to an act of love. The gospels favour silent giving, thereby delinking the act of giving with doership, as does the *Gita*. "When you give to the needy, do not let your left hand know what your right hand is doing," says Gospel of Matthew (6:3).

Satirist Thomas Carlyle said, on giving: "The work an unknown good man has done is like a vein of water flowing hidden underground, secretly making the ground green." If you take a cue from this, you would dissociate your names from your charities and give silently. If, as a corporate giver, you are unable to give anonymously, then it seems philanthropy is making you neither a karma yogi nor a seeker on the path of transcendence from the material to the spiritual.

Expectation Brings Frustration

Osho

f you expect too much, you will be frustrated. If you don't want to be frustrated, don't expect. Live without expectations and there will be no frustration. But people go on expecting; then frustration comes in — frustration is the shadow of expectation. When you feel frustrated you think that existence is doing something wrong to you. Any asking is asking too much. Don't ask, be. And then you will be surprised — whatsoever happens is good; you have no way to judge it.

I used to stay with a rich family in Calcutta. Once I went; the family had come to take me from the airport. The husband was very sad.

I enquired, "What is the matter?"

He said, "There has been a great loss."

Listening to this, his wife started laughing.

She said, "Don't bother about what he says. There has been no loss — in fact, there has been a great profit."

I was puzzled.

I said, "You both are here. Please try to explain this riddle to me."

The wife said, "There is no riddle. He was expecting Rs.10 lakh and he got only Rs.5 lakh. So he says, 'Rs.5 lakh loss', and I say, You have profited' — but he won't listen, and he is very sad."

When you expect Rs.10 lakh and you get Rs.5 lakh you feel frustrated. If you are not expecting and you get Rs.5 lakh you are full of joy, thankfulness, gratitude.

Don't expect, and you see your whole life becomes a joy. Expect, and your whole life becomes a hell. Expectation is the cause. If you want to change, never start by the effect, start by the cause. Frustration is the effect. You can go on fighting with frustration — nothing will happen, you will become more and more frustrated. Whenever you are feeling miserable, go into it and find out where the cause is. If you want to drop the effect then avoid the cause; then become aware, more and more aware.

61

There are many people who enjoy frustration. There are many people who enjoy being miserable. In fact, they cannot tolerate happiness at all. When they are miserable they are happy, when they are happy they feel very miserable. Whenever you are miserable you gain something: sympathy, attention. Whenever you are happy nobody shows any sympathy — in fact, people become jealous. When you are unhappy everybody is a friend, everybody sympathizes with you — even your enemy will sympathize with you. When you are happy even your friend will become jealous and inimical.

When you are happy nobody pays any attention to you. People avoid you. In fact, they start thinking you must be mad: Happy? Who has ever heard of anybody being happy! When you are unhappy they accept you. Then they think everything is okay, because this is how things have to be. And people enjoy your unhappiness, that's why they pay attention — because whenever you are unhappy they can compare themselves, and deep down they can feel good.

You love frustration? Then go into it. Become more artistic about it, decorate it a little more; make new possibilities, new doors to become more frustrated. If you don't enjoy it, then I don't see the problem. Just go deep into it, watch, and you will find some expectation hidden behind. Whenever you expect, you are asking for frustration. Drop expectations!

Show More Understanding

Rajinder Singh Ji

here is a story of a holy man from the Middle East who was in the habit of not eating breakfast until a hungry person came by to share it with him. One day an elderly man came by. The holy man saw him and invited him to share his breakfast with him. The elderly man thanked him profusely and sat down at the table to join him.

As they began to say a blessing over the food, the elderly man said aloud a prayer to the pagan gods. The holy man was taken aback since he only believed in one God. He felt that the elderly man was a non-believer and so he became very upset.

"If you believe in pagans, then I don't want you in my house!" he said to the old man, who scurried off.

When the holy man returned to his table, he heard God speak to him.

God said, "What right have you to send that man away?"

The holy man said, "He did not believe in you."

God replied, "Look here! I know he does not believe in me. But I have been supplying the unbeliever with food every day for 80 years even though he doesn't believe in me. Couldn't you tolerate him for one single meal?"

We sometimes become righteous about our own beliefs and our own goodness and look down upon others. Who is good and who is bad? No matter how bad we think someone is, God provides for everyone. There are people who lie, who cheat, who deceive others, and who slander others. There are people who hurt others and even kill others. It takes all types to make the world. Some of us believe in God, others don't; still others are agnostics. Yet, God provides life to each of them. No one is perfect.

Even those of us who are on the spiritual path feel righteous about ourselves. Some people criticize others who do not meditate as much as they do, who do not do as much service as they do, or who do not live by the ethical values as well as they do. Sometimes people become very outspoken about the faults of others. But have we ever analysed our own selves? Is it our duty to become reformers of others? We should accept the fact that no one is without fault. God knows everyone's faults. God sees everything we do and everything everyone else does.

We should be kind and loving to all. We should respect and learn to live amicably with people who have different beliefs and customs from those that we have. Why be critical of non-believers and agnostics? Are we not entitled to believe in what we are convinced about, as long as we do not hurt anyone? God has made a world with people following many different religions and yet provides for each of them. Each one of us is different; this fact alone should enable us to show more understanding to those who do not agree with us.

When we show love and understanding to all, then we are acting like true children of the Lord. God is love, and when we show love for others, we too are filled with love and come closer to God.

Balance Your Intelligence

Osho

The balance of intelligence is the essence of yoga. Generally our mind is always swaying in extremes. Either we are in one extreme, or we go to the other extreme. Either we love somebody madly or we start hating him madly. Either we are madly after money, or we are crazy about renouncing it. It seems very difficult to remain in the middle. Making a friend is easy and making an enemy is also easy; but to remain in the middle of friendship and enmity is extremely difficult for us. And the one, who stays in the middle, attains to balance.

Balanced intelligence means to balance despite duality. If you are a shopkeeper weighing goods on scale, you would know that when both sides become evenly balanced and the indicator of the scale stays exactly in the centre — when it is tilting towards neither the left nor right — then the balanced intelligence is attained.

Krishna says, "The essence of yoga is balanced intelligence." Krishna says, I call that man a yogi who has attained balance of intelligence. He breaks his identity with the sides of the scale and stands where the scale stops, where the equilibrium is gained, where the middle point is attained. He stays in the middle of two extremes; finds exactly the middle point; he is neither a friend, nor an enemy; he stops in the middle.

Whenever the preparation to move from one side to the other side starts, stop moving to the other side — do not be in haste. Do not go to the other side. If you are in anger, then just stay with anger; do not be in a haste to go over to repentance. But the moment anger arises; the mind immediately starts putting its other step on the side of repentance. One half of a man does anger and the other half starts preparing itself for doing repentance. Observe a man in anger. If you notice his face you will find mixed expressions. He is getting angry but at the same time he is also hesitating and preparing for repentance.

Sometimes when you are standing after a shower, your weight is resting on one leg. Close your eyes and try to concentrate and find out whether your weight is resting on the left leg or on the right leg. And if you find that the weight is resting on the left leg, then stop and keep on observing it. After some time you will find that the weight has been shifted to the right leg. And if the weight is on the right leg, then also keep on standing and seeing inside that the weight is on the right leg. At once you will find the weight has shifted to the left side. The mind is changing so fast inside. It does not stay on a leg even for a second. From the left it goes to the right; from the right to the left. Bring yourself to a state in which your weight is neither on the left leg, nor on the right leg; rather it comes in the middle of both the legs. If you get a glimpse of this even for a second, you will be surprised. And the moment you come to know it is in the middle, at the same moment you will feel the body is no more. At once you will experience absolute bodylessness.

Shaking off the Past

Deepak M Ranade

 wise man was participating in a conversation. He contributed by telling the group a joke. All those present were highly amused and appreciated the humour. After a while, he narrated the joke again. This time the response was more tempered. After some time, he said it the third time and it evoked barely any response. When he tried repeating it a fourth time, a member of the group burst out: "Why are you repeating the joke so many times? It's no longer amusing; it's irritating!"

The wise man responded: "If repeating a joke ceases to amuse after a few times, then how do we carry on with repeated remembrance of painful stories?"

The way a person deals with unpleasantness in the past influences largely, his attitude and approach to dealing with the present. Carrying excess emotional baggage does not augur well; it could affect your self-esteem. You might get convinced that you are at the root of all the misfortunes that have befallen you and will mope and indulge in an unforgiving criticism of yourself. The already low levels of self-esteem could ebb further and make you cynical.

Embers of unpleasant memories get fanned by self-pity and self-criticism and so the flame of sorrow is kept alive. It is akin to being a jury at one's own trial and about being obsessive about fixing the blame rather than the problem. Moving on with life after an unsavoury incident requires one to view it as just one among many events and incidents in one's life.

Que sera sera — whatever will be will be. Reminiscing and reacting to the past is as futile as attempting to resuscitate a corpse. Most people try and strive to uproot the weeds of unpleasant memories. This is not possible as selective amnesia is still in the domain of science fiction. The memories will remain and one needs to let them be. It is far more important not to be reactive about the long buried past and to not use that as a scale to measure oneself. The past should never be empowered to affect the present. Passing a verdict about oneself based entirely on past events deals a body blow to growth and development.

Every event is the outcome of a host of complex factors, most of which are not entirely predictable or controllable. The possibility thinker is positive and has faith in himself believing that any dream is possible. The probability thinker, in contrast, is a sceptical individual teeming with self-doubt and fearing the probability of failure.

A farmer had a couple of horses that he used for tilling his land. They would be tied the whole day to plough the field or draw water from the well to irrigate the fields. At night the farmer would leave the rope tied round their necks but never bothered to tie the other end. It was free.

An onlooker enquired "Why don't you tie the other end? Won't the animal run away?"

The farmer replied, "The end around their necks is enough to make them believe that they are captive. They are convinced that the other end is secured."

The unsavoury memories of the past should not become such convictions that bind us and restrict our freedom to evolve and grow. Treat the present as a 'present', a gift free of the past. Let's wake up to dream about the wonderful future that beckons us.

Why Must I Forgive?

MPK Kutty

he call to forgiveness and reconciliation is vital for the survival of the human race. "Forgiveness is the key that unlocks the door of resentment and the handcuffs of hate. It is a power that breaks the chains of bitterness and the shackles of selfishness," wrote Corrie ten Boom, a Holocaust survivor.

Our capacity to forgive indicates our moral likeness to the One who commanded us to forgive and who freely forgives us. "Father, forgive them for they know not what they do," pleaded Jesus as he endured the Cross.

The 2,000-year-old plea continues to be the subject of meditation for Christians as they observe Lent every year. The example set by Jesus is the cardinal doctrine built into the faith — that of forgiveness. The day of crucifixion, observed as Good Friday, is a reminder to reflect and learn to forgive. The death and resurrection of Jesus Christ was but fulfilment of a prophesy that a Messiah would arrive to intercede for the sins of the human race and would rescue them from the power of darkness and bring them into the Kingdom of Light. Had the Roman soldiers known that they were crucifying the 'Lord of Glory' they would have averted it.

Jesus provided a new way - - the way of Grace — that whoever believes in His atoning sacrifice on the Cross would receive forgiveness and salvation. Through the work of Jesus Christ the seeker discovers the love of God and the forgiveness of God. This transference from darkness to light, from slavery to freedom and from condemnation to forgiveness is all implied in the atoning death of Jesus on the Cross and his resurrection.

The cause of many a suffering is the feeling of vengeance, jealousy and greed, yet we have a choice before us, to not succumb to these negative aspects. By forgiving those who wrong us, not only do we create the right environment for harmony and peace, we also promote physical, mental and spiritual well-being.

Miracles happen when two alienated people start all over again. An estranged father holds out his hand to his daughter; those on the brink of divorce suddenly undergo a change of heart; bitter enemies become friends as suspicions get lifted — transforming relationships happen through the melting away of bitterness and animosity.

When Jesus directed his followers to love their enemies and to forgive offenders 'seventy times-seven' he was prescribing not only ways of protecting their souls, but also their bodies from various illnesses that arise out of anger and frustration. Forgiveness is an act of love. It has the power to heal. The life of Jesus is an example of the fact that at the heart of love is forgiveness and compassion. Forgiveness creates the possibilities of release from an unfair or unpleasant past. It takes us off the escalator of revenge providing an escape from gradual and total ruin. To forgive is to put down heavy baggage from one's back. It is setting oneself free from bonds of hatred.

Today when terrorism and hatred, suspicion and greed seek to create chaos and uncertainty all over the globe, understanding, atonement and forgiveness need to be propagated and practised more effectively if we are to improve the quality of our lives and evolve on the spiritual path. Forgiveness holds the key. Its give and take that will open doors to greater brotherhood and understanding, and renew hopes in the hearts of those who live in remembrance of what Good Friday stands for.

Spiritual Intelligence

Vijay Vancheswar

onventional intelligence is linked to the capability of an individual to assimilate and convey facts as well as manage challenging situations. Intelligence Quotient, IQ, measures the brain's ability to grasp, retain and recall factual knowledge. Emotional Intelligence, EQ, measures the ability to understand and maturely manage people and challenges. Spiritual Intelligence, SI, expands the horizon beyond the ego. It attunes one to a larger circle of awareness and influence. Spiritually evolved people remain connected with a sense of universal oneness. This enables them to respond to trying situations and issues in a remarkably composed manner.

The first-hand experience of MK Gandhi of the social injustice prevalent under the racial regime of apartheid is a case in point. Louis Fischer in his biography of Gandhi, recounts what Gandhi thought was the most creative experience of his life as the night that he spent crouched and shivering in the cold at the Maritzburg rail station in Natal, South Africa, unable to even reach for his own overcoat while empathizing with a poor black family who were thrown out of a train.

This incident transformed Gandhi's level of awareness, attuning him to a larger purpose in life. Spiritual intelligence transcends the realm of objective knowledge and one's own identity. It invokes a sense of oneness across all forms of life. However, success in higher learning and knowledge assimilation runs the risk of promoting one's sense of importance and superiority. This can only be avoided if we acknowledge the existence of a higher power.

Ramana Maharshi regarded the illiterate as being more fortunate as they are less likely to be victims of pride and egoism that comes from reading and writing — as it happens with some. Spiritual scientist Albert Einstein states that the main purpose of education should be to bring morality in actions and subdue one's ego. Ramakrishna Paramahamsa was hardly educated. Yet the most

71

erudite and scholarly felt humbled in his presence. Many a time we tend to ignore simple solutions to life's challenges. Warren Buffett, the celebrated businessman, captures the significance of simplicity when he says, "There seems to be a perverse human characteristic that likes to make easy things difficult!"

Einstein said, "Not all that counts in life can be counted and not all that can be counted counts," which aptly captures this truth.

Abiding by the philosophy of simple living and high thinking can help us tap and deploy the innate resource of spiritual intelligence within. Responding to the demands of life using spiritual intelligence paves the way for a deeper awareness of the cosmic consciousness linking all of humanity. To energize this intelligence, it is important that we cajole the mind to go within instead of its habitual tendency to focus outwards.

Connecting intuitively to the core of our being promotes the expression of our spirit. Intuitive wisdom can provide remarkably simple solutions to many complex challenges of life. It makes us more receptive to the power of wisdom that is always available within and around us. Steadily, but surely, we can then abide by the wise counsel for peaceful and happy living, "Let sincerity and not seriousness be the guiding basis for all our actions and responses in life."

Search for Perfect Master

Swami Sukhabodhananda

ost of us are caught up searching for the perfect master. But the question one has to ask is: Am I the right student? If not, then one can never learn from the perfect master. "What shall I do in order to be enlightened," asked the student.

"As much as you can do to make the sun rise or set," replied the master.

"Then what is the use of all the spiritual practices," asked the student.

"Only to make sure you are awake when the sun rises and the sun sets", replied the master.

To be inwardly awake is the quality of wise living. To search for being the right student is the right step to be wise. There are three types of impacts: environmental, experiential and educational. Most of us are controlled and bullied by the environment and experience. But if we can bring in the quality of education in our experiences, then we will not be a doormat. With the power of spiritual education, we can grow and learn from environment and experience. In ordinary situations with the power of spiritual education we can have extraordinary insights.

When you face a situation or look at the Earth, are you responding out of love, silence or are you reacting out of anger and disappointment? To be reflective on one's state of being when one meets the Earth or situations of life is being a right student. Or in other words are you reacting or responding to the situation and learning to respond is a part of wise studentship.

As you become aware of how you are dealing with the situations of life, you have to look little more deeply and discover that there is a distinction between the social self and essential self.

Our identity is defined by society. For example, if I am considered a good speaker, who has given me this title? So our identity is defined by society and hence we are so dependent on society. The remote control of our life is with society. This keeps us in bondage. In most cases society controls and dominates our lives. Thus a social self in us is born.

If one is spiritual, then this conflict is a spiritual problem. If we search within, we find that there is an essential self. This essential self is who we are and not what others want of us. If one can recognize this distinction and go little deeper, one operates from the essential self and keep the social self on the peripheral.

The essential self has energy which unites, like love, gratitude, which keep us in order and harmony. Anger and jealousy create disorder and hence are not essential.

Keeping the essential as one's centre, one has to deal with earth, the situations of life. So often the situations of life are disturbing. One has to learn new ways to love, new ways to learn, and new ways to enjoy those situations. By doing so one logs on to powerful self which will be supportive and not destructive. A self which learns to love, learn and enjoy is supportive. Ego which reacts to situations, does not learn and enjoy the challenges of the situations lives life as a nuisance. To discard the ego which is a nuisance value and to install the self that is essential is a part of wise living. So don't get lost in search for the perfect master. But instead be a right student.

Turn Traffic Jams around

Shri Nimishananda Ashram

We are moving along with the current of our desires, our own goals, aims and agendas. In the process, we tend to get bogged down by problems and feel fed up with things in general, resulting in stress, strain and tension. We are constantly thinking of negative things, having a sense of fear unnecessarily and constantly expecting the worst to happen. Negativity and adversities are attracted by our negative state of being and they come and settle in us, making our mind a garbage bin. Many a times we feel that everybody is victimizing us for no fault of ours, making us feel very pathetic and ordinary.

Instead, when we don't unnecessarily assume and presume the above, we value and feel that life is precious, auspicious, esteemed and extraordinary. Meditation brings about this awareness to make our life extraordinary. When you firmly value that practice of meditation is extraordinary, then, faith, trust, belief and will power empowers you to lead an extraordinary life. These activate and expand the bandwidth of your free will and wisdom and further infuse you with inspiration and enthusiasm. Now you will start transforming mundane circumstances to extraordinary occasions.

Savour every moment of your life, even when it brings unexpected challenges to you, by treating them not as problems that obstruct your progress, but as opportunities that foster your growth. Let us say that you are cooking a dish and it gets completely spoilt. Don't worry. Cook it once more if you can or cater it from outside. Don't brood over it and invite tension. Remember, for an extraordinary mind, the solutions are always striking and simple. When there is no interest, life remains mechanical and ordinary but when you are deeply interested in everything you do, every situation becomes a doorway to expansion.

Your life becomes extraordinarily joyful. The external world hardly cares whether you are laughing, crying, bored or suffering, but your internal world is always in your hands. Make it beautiful and extraordinary. When you enjoy every circumstance as extraordinary, the unpleasant elements of stress, strain and tension that torments each day of your present existence disappears completely. Never waste a single moment of your life in boredom and depression. These negative factors slowly choke off the bliss of your soul along with peace, contentment and creativity.

Even if you are caught in a traffic jam, relax and enjoy the respite from driving. Resolve that "I will now convert this traumatic situation into a blissful one." Then, evolve by chanting a mantra, singing a *bhajan* or praying for someone whom you think is suffering. Then, you convert an ordinary moment into an extraordinary moment of presence of mind and wisdom. So, rejuvenate and refresh your soul. Don't worry about the traffic ahead or behind. Till the traffic moves, you cannot move, anyway! So, just relax and use this time to touch your inner core; accept the traffic jam as being inevitable.

However, if you have the habit of losing your cool in traffic jams, sorrow becomes your constant companion. Even if the delay means that you will miss an important appointment, don't allow this to stress you because it saps your enthusiasm and power to overcome obstacles. A truly extraordinary life is touching base with our soul through meditation and maintaining silence daily. This expands the inner self and makes it blossom to attain emancipation and liberation from an ordinary, apprehensive life to an extraordinary, valuable, blissful life.

Instruments of Peace

Dadi Janki

n my early morning meditations, I can hear the call of the world for peace — not just for an end to conflict, but for a deep, inner stillness and calm, which we remember as our original state. To find peace, first we must teach ourselves to become quiet; only then we can become peaceful. Becoming peaceful means to seize the reins of mind and bring runaway thoughts to a halt. Once we have the mind's attention, we can begin to coax it to take us into silence, a true silence; not the place without sound, but the place in which we experience a deep sense of peace and a pervasive awareness of our well-being.

To move into this state of profound silence, we must train the intellect to create pure, good thoughts and to concentrate. Our wasteful thoughts burden us. Our habits of creating too many thoughts and words exhaust the intellect. We must ask, "How can I cultivate the habit of pure thought?"

Who is it that yearns to go into silence? It is I, the inner being, the soul. As I detach from my body and from bodily things, and turn away from the distractions of the world, I can face inwards to the inner being. Like a perfectly calm lake when all whispers of wind have stopped, the inner being shimmers, quietly reflecting the intrinsic qualities of the soul. Feelings of peace and well-being steal across my mind and, with them, thoughts of benevolence.

I let go of all thoughts of discontentment and am reminded of my oldest, most intrinsic state of being. I remember this inner calm. Though I have not been here recently, I remember it as my most fundamental awareness, and a feeling of happiness and contentment wells up inside of me. In this state I know every soul to be my friend. I am my own friend. I am deeply quiet. I am silent and utterly at peace. This deep well of peace is the original state of the soul. When I am in this state, I feel the flow of love for humanity and I feel a state more elevated than what I would normally call happiness, a state of bliss. It is when I attain this state that something truly miraculous

77

can happen. When I am in this state of complete soul-conscious rest, I become aware that energy is beginning to flow into me. I feel strength and a power so expansive, that in this moment I know there is nothing I cannot do, nowhere I cannot reach.

When this happens, I am experiencing the connection with the divine energy and the flow of God's power into my inner being. If I stay focused inwards, connected with this stream of divine power, even the way I use the physical senses will be different. When I look at the world, I will see through my original nature of benevolence and experience compassion for the world.

It is this power that transforms me inside, making me pure and powerful. When the soul and God are linked together, there is a power that reaches me and invisibly across to others, bringing about transformation in them, in nature, and in the world. The secret of this power of silence is that I don't have to do the work of transformation. Divine power automatically transforms. Let me do the inner work. Let me go deeply into that experience of the original state of the self, and let there be silence so that God is able to do His work through me, His instrument.

Mango as Spiritual Guide

Lama Doboom Tulku

his is the mango season. That has set me thinking...Acharya Nagarjuna is a great Indian philosopher. Many traditions regard him as a Tantric Acharya, in some other traditions he is regarded as an Ayurvedic expert and in yet others, even an Alchemist, but I am yet to come across a story of his being associated with horticulture. I will not be surprised if I discover that some traditions believe him to be a horticulturist. But as far as his knowledge about the mango is concerned it is universally accepted that what he says is but natural and common wisdom.

Nagarjuna in his letter talks to the king about different categories of mangoes. They are special varieties whose appearances and degrees of ripening can be categorized as follows: 1) those not ripe but appear ripe; 2) those ripe but appear not ripe; 3) those unripe and appear unripe; and 4) those ripe and appear ripe. He was extrapolating this with reference to people we come across in our daily lives.

In terms of preference, obviously the kind of mango we must choose is the one belonging to the last category, as it is ready to be served and there is no risk of waste involved. The second preference should be given to, in my opinion, to the second last. Because it does not deceive you, you can just discard it right away or wait for it to ripen. Then the next in order of selection should be the one mentioned in number two. It involves some chances of waste but at least you can use it after some testing before cutting to see if it is really ripe.

The one you must avoid is the first category of mangoes. Choice of the mangoes in any case is not a big deal and much insignificant, in comparison to the selection of people whether it is a matter of a *kalayanamitra* or spiritual friend, or an associate in mundane affairs. These days if we look around, there is no dearth of people who are likened by Nagarjuna to the first category of mangoes. They are those who have acquired special tricks to project themselves as friends. They cannot only be risky for spiritual path seekers but also to the society as a whole.

Spiritual friends should not only be spiritually ripe but should also appear to be so. They must be morally clean, compassionate, have association with good people. People promoting themselves as spiritual gurus with tricks are particularly dangerous. There is great chance of getting themselves corrupted, if already not corrupted, by name, fame, wealth and position. In mundane areas also, a friend should be an upright person, with clear mind and wisdom.

A friend can be depended upon as your *mitra* not because of your position or money power. It is not necessary that your friend or for that matter a political leader is a rhetoric speaker or writer. It is the inner values of the person that count. This will remain true as long as the values placed on honesty and truthfulness have not vanished from this earth. And the reason why one should believe that is because all of us know the ripe mango which is both ripe and looks ripe enough for you to select, will always be preferred.

There's Heaven on Earth

Marguerite Theophil

arth is crammed with heaven. Sadly, though, earning a living, raising families and achieving success, most of us hardly take notice of this. It takes poets, or those with poetic ears, eyes and tongues to reconnect us to this state of noticing.

"Crammed with heaven" is that just-right phrase from the poet Elizabeth Barrett Browning: "Earth's crammed with heaven, And every common bush afire with God; But only he who sees, takes off his shoes..."

Once we learn to see with the eyes of the heart, or what Islamic mystics have called *chasm-e-dil,* we begin to inhabit a world transformed by our seeing. The bland or unattractive reveals hidden beauty, the ordinary becomes sacred, everyday events take on new meaning and depth.

Alice Walker's novel, *The Color Purple,* with its story of suffering graced with love, and earthy wisdom of its poor African American characters, is a powerful if unlikely sacred text, to be read and re-read. The main character, the simple, unlettered Celie, often thought of God and scribbled notes to Him, but in the middle of a sad and difficult life, she stops writing. Celie meets Shug, an unlikely wise teacher, in the form of a sassy, sultry singer with unusual ideas, who teaches her that God does not have to be an old white man with a grey beard but that He — or 'It' as Shug refers to God saying God is neither man or woman — can be seen in everyone else without the help of the white man's religious teaching. Celie's final letter, after not writing to God for a very long time, begins, "Dear God, dear stars, dear trees, dear sky, dear peoples. Dear everything. Dear God."

The Color Purple has another startling teaching — startling in the way it is phrased. Shug declares: "I think it pisses God off if you walk by the colour purple in a field somewhere and don't notice it."

Later she adds by way of explanation: "People think pleasing God is all God cares about. But any fool living in the world can see it always trying to please us back…always making little surprises and springing them on us when we least expect it."

Viktor Frankl, author of the popular *Man's Search For Meaning* — tells of catching a glimpse of heaven even at a Nazi death camp, in the midst of unimaginable horrors, degradation and inhumanity. He writes of how, standing outside late one evening, "…we saw sinister clouds glowing in the west and the whole sky alive with clouds of ever-changing shapes and colours, from steel blue to blood red. The desolate grey mud huts provided a sharp contrast, while the puddles on the muddy ground reflected the glowing sky. Then, after minutes of moving silence, one prisoner said to another, "How beautiful the world could be!"

Reminders are found everywhere. Tracy Chapman sings in her hauntingly beautiful voice:

You can look to the stars in search of the answers,

Look for God and life on distant planets,

Have your faith in the ever after,

While each of us holds inside the map to the labyrinth,

And heaven's here on earth.

This living can be heaven or hell, depending on the perspectives that guide the choices that we make for ourselves and others, every single day of our lives.

Live Life with Compassion

Purnima

ompassion is not an attribute of any one religion. It is a universal principle for happiness and peace. In a world torn by conflict and strife, where violence and not love dictates people's actions, what every person, at every level, of every age needs to learn is the art of nurturing compassion within. Be it a homemaker fulfilling the many needs of her family, an entrepreneur meeting people and clinching deals for her company, a politician passing Bills in the legislature that can change the destiny of millions or an autorickshaw driver bargaining for higher rates with his passenger — whoever you may be, you need compassion. Compassion should no more lie in the ideologies of philosophers, or in the lucrative rewards of theologians (in the afterlife). The voice of compassion needs to be heard in every household, educational institution, office, business unit, shop, mall and theatre, besides other places and circumstances.

For centuries now we have reserved compassion to be a prerogative of a chosen few, like a Christ or a Buddha. We have also conceptually dismissed the possibility of someone living and embodying such a quality in the hurly-burly of everyday life. Is it so difficult to live compassionately? Or are we so incapable that we cannot raise ourselves to those standards?

Compassion begins with empathy. Empathy is the ability to feel for another. Those who are sensitive to the motions of life, to the experiences of pain and pleasure, are capable of empathy. Those who have watched the movements of their thoughts, the burden of unnecessary thinking, and the pain of conflicting thoughts know it well. Those who have paid attention to their emotional upsurges, the unintelligent ways of anger, hurt or hate, the irrationality of fear, feel empathy for another who is going through a similar emotion. Hence, compassion begins with attention to one's own life experiences, be it physical or emotional.

Empathy and compassion thus born would naturally blossom into acts of kindness to reach out to others. Well-being of the other is the highest priority for a compassionate person; hence her actions would reflect tremendous intelligence, fortitude and discretion. It could be a dynamic plunge into action to change the adverse situation of the one who is suffering. It could also be gentle words of love and strength or a heartfelt prayer for Divine help.

Compassion is not the armour of the weak; it is the weapon of the strong. It is irresponsible to think, believe and preach that anger and violence can solve our problems. Problems at micro as well as macro level arise because of lack of understanding and love between people. Problems that are situation-based are very less compared to those that are emotion based. Situation-based problems need better strategy and skill to solve them but emotion-based problems need people who are involved in moving out of those negative emotions that are causing them. That is why any constructive change can never be effected through anger and violence. Compassion is the answer. Let us nurture the noble virtue of compassion consciously with dedication. Let us see the faces of people who walk into our world with smiles, tears, affection and wrath. Let us meditate on their feelings to let compassion blossom.

It's Good to Forget

Maulana Wahiduddin Khan

Everyday people face negative experiences. Whether of greater or lesser import, people generally like to dwell on these negative experiences. Once this becomes a habit, it has a negative effect. Then unpleasant experiences become a part of their active memory, till it becomes a jungle of negativity. So it is best to forget these kinds of sad events.

In your case, whatever happened was beyond your control, but it is in your hands to forget it and prevent it from becoming a part of your memory. If others are not ready to take your advice on this, you had better become its first follower.

What is education? Education is not just the means of making you a degree holder; it is the gateway to the art of living. Education enables you to think, to discover the principles of life, and to correctly evaluate your experiences. Education gives you the ability to know the difference between the achievable and unachievable. If you are an educated person in this sense, you will certainly discover the value of the habit of forgetting.

The choice in this context is not between forgetting and not forgetting: the real choice is between living with all kinds of bitter memories and totally freeing yourself from them. Try to forget unpleasant memories, for the alternative to this is living in bitterness and that is not a good choice for anyone.

The habit — of forgetting — leads you to many good things. It saves you from distraction, it economizes your energy, it prevents you from wasting your time, and it shields you from negative thoughts. All these things are so important for a better life that any sacrifice to achieve it is certainly worth it.

In life your share is only 50 per cent. The rest of the 50 per cent is supplied by others. Living with bitter memories means that you are not ready to accept this law of nature. You cannot change the law of nature, so change yourself. This will give you the gift of a comfortable life in every situation.

If you are not ready to forget what is forgettable, then after sometime you will become addicted to this habit. Bitter memory is fed by bad experiences and so you tend to recall them everyday. This is a very bad sign. This will create a permanent obstacle to the development of your personality.

Of the two kinds of memories, good and bad, the former gives you energy, while the latter ruins your life. You have to appreciate this difference and try to live with good memories and forget the bad memories. This habit will help you achieve a good human life.

Memory is an integral part of your mind. There is no escape from memory. The only option is to try not to make memory a part of your conscious mind, but relegate it to the unconscious mind. And the forgetting habit serves that very purpose. We cannot delete our memory from our minds, but we can make it ineffective by storing it in the memory archives.

Memory when good is a positive guide, and when bad, totally negative. You have to control your memory rather than be controlled by it. Make your memory your intellectual storehouse and not the master of your daily conduct.

The Thirst for Fame

Sudhamahi Regunathan

enerally everything in life comes in pairs. Not in terms of opposites but in terms of ensuring balance in existence. Like rights come with duty, freedom comes with responsibility and so on. The secret is to identify the pairs. Some of them are visible and taken for granted. For some others, you have to play something like a memory game...you have to search out the pair. When any concept is understood along with its pair then it becomes firmly rooted and gives more results than when it is tackled or pursued in isolation.

One such single which is hunting for its pair is fame. Most people seek fame. Some want international recognition and work towards that, some want national acclaim and yet others are happy being the leader in the family circle or the colony community. Again the reason for the fame and the talent being showcased can be as varied as flowers in a garden. To celebrate the idea of fame we also have many record books that document the first ever in different fields.

Our quest for fame is perhaps only younger than our quest for truth. Psychologists say that every human being seeks immortality and therefore seeks fame...so that they live beyond their calendar years, at least in name. And that is why there is the obsession to 'become'.

Fame brings immediate power. Sometimes the power of fame may not bring any wealth. But it brings honour and respect. What makes the fame lasting? What pairs with fame? Much too often fame is confused with the riches it might bring. It is believed that if money is made, dignity and respect will naturally accrue. That is not entirely untrue. Money does buy many things...but that which is bought, also sells, is it not? As the market decides the price for such things, the halo of fame remains, but the substance that makes it, in terms of adulation and trust that the famous inspire, gets whittled down. On looking a little closer one finds that, since the power wielded by fame is derived from it, lasting fame will accrue only when you recognize from whom you have derived that power and invest it back in them or that. Sacred books live eternally because they invest the reader with the power of divine blessing. Leaders derive their power from the people, parents from their children, a cook from the people who savour his food, a designer from his craftsmen and so it goes, in every field of life.

The pair of fame is thus service, which is to be useful. When there is service, fame comes automatically and this fame is rooted in a noble activity. To remember this is the path to the kind of fame that lives after you is what makes you immortal. That is why a good teacher is remembered at all times and is 'famous' among students of the school and their families.

The Sanskrit tradition identified long ago that the eternal quality of fame and the dignity it inspires is oft-smudged by the grime of life. What remains and dominates all actions is the desire for fame. So it is said humorously in a *subhashitani* (a couplet which has an inherent lesson in it) that break a pot, tear your clothes and ride a donkey, if you may, but make sure you become famous — at any cost! But surely, not at the cost of crossing the thin line that divides fame from notoriety?

The Blooming of a Lotus

Thich Nhat Hanh

he function of meditation practice is to heal and transform. It helps us to be whole, and to look deeply into ourselves and around us in order to realize what is really there. The energy that is used in meditation is mindfulness; to look deeply into the heart of things in order to see their true nature. When mindfulness is present, meditation is present. Mindfulness helps us to understand the true essence of the object of meditation — whether it is a perception, an emotion, an action, a reaction, the presence of a person or object.

By looking deeply, the meditation practitioner gains insight, *prajna*, or wisdom. This insight has the power to liberate us from our own suffering and bondage. In the meditation process, fetters are undone, internal blocks of suffering such as fear, anger, despair and hatred get removed, relationships with humans and nature become easier, and there is freedom and joy. We become aware of what is inside us and around us; we are fresher, and we become more alive in our daily existence. As we become freer and happier, we cease to act in ways that make others suffer, and we are able to bring about change around us and to help others become free. Isn't that wonderful?

The one who practices meditation is like a lotus flower in the process of blooming. Buddhas are fully bloomed human flowers, beautiful and refreshing. All of us are Buddhas-to-be. That is why in practice centres when people meet each other, they form a lotus with their palms and greet each other while bowing, saying, 'a lotus for you, a Buddha-to-be'. As they inhale while saying 'a lotus for you' and exhale, smiling, while saying 'a Buddha-to-be', they have the appearance of a blooming flower.

It may be possible for you to meditate on your own, without a teacher or a Sangha, namely, Buddhist community of practice. But it goes without saying that to practise with a teacher and a Sangha is more advisable and much easier. A teacher is someone who has had the experience of the practice, and has succeeded in it. A Sangha is a meditation community where everyone follows more or less the same kind of practice. Since everyone is doing the same practice, it becomes easier for you to practise too, because the group energy emitted by the Sangha is strong and very supportive. You can also learn a great deal from individual members of the Sangha, especially those who have realized some degree of peace and transformation. There are many things you may find difficult to do when alone, but in the presence of the Sangha you can do them easily. All of us who have practised with a Sangha can testify to this fact...

In the Buddhist tradition, we consider Sangha one of the three gems. The three gems are Buddha, Dharma and Sangha. As we see it, the three gems are already in your heart. The Sangha in yourself may guide you to the Sangha that is somewhere near you. Maybe the teacher and the Sangha are right there, very close to you, but you have not yet noticed. With practice, you will generate the energy of mindfulness, which may lead you towards a teacher and a community.

The Power of Truth

Murali A Raghavan

t is said that if a man speaks truth uninterruptedly for 12 years, whatever he speaks thereafter will come true. The saying, at once, reveals the power of truth as also the difficulty of remaining conscious of truth consistently for any length of time.

Theoretically speaking, truth should be a simple task as the most natural thing to do. Truth about oneself is always self-evident. Our thoughts and feelings, fears and aspirations, likes and dislikes are known to us and yet, we hardly express ourselves fully and truthfully. Instead, we battle with our conscience, concoct stories and manipulate our expressions to camouflage our thoughts and true feelings. We choose the hard option driven by all sorts of fears: fear of being found out, of rejection, of losing honour, status and image. As long as the veneer lasts it is fine but the foundation underneath remains ever brittle and shaky.

Seers who reached the summit of existence have done so as they have boldly ventured onto the path of truth with conscience as their sole guide. Gandhiji's uncompromising attitude towards truth is what made him a *mahatma*. In his autobiographical work, *My Experiments with Truth,* he unabashedly confesses his innermost thoughts and feelings, weaknesses and failings, adducing that 'if something is shameful to reveal, it is more shameful to hide'. Those who did not know him called him a half-naked *fakir.* But this frail man, partially-clad in a skimpy dhoti but fully clothed in the attire of truth, was more powerful than battalions of armed men dressed in uniform.

In the *Ramayana,* there are many instances where the miraculous power of truth is revealed. Sita boldly proclaims that if she has been truthful and chaste, Hanuman's tail that was set afire by enemies would not scorch him. The fire god had no option but to bow before the truth. Hanuman's tail remained unharmed despite the raging fire. Again, towards the end of the epic, Sita is asked to prove her chastity before an assembly. This was the second such instance after the fire-ordeal she was made to undergo soon after the war. Mother Earth, unable to bear the travesty of justice, opened up and took her daughter back into her womb.

In more recent times, a distraught middle-aged woman came sobbing and fell at the feet of Kanchi Mahaswami. The compassionate saint blessed her as was his wont, and said, *"Sowbhagyavati bhava"* — May you enjoy a long and happy married life. The startled woman informed him that she had just received the news of her husband's death on the war front. Upon hearing this, the swami said the words came from him spontaneously and, hence, should be presumed to be God's decree. News arrives that the woman's husband was taken prisoner and that his return was imminent.

Truth is immortal. A shadow of lie can temporarily dim its illumination but only in passing. Lies, however, have a limited life and need to continuously breed and proliferate to keep up the pretence of constancy. Truth is like fresh water, cleansing the mind of sensory debris like desire, hatred, greed, jealousy, envy and animosity. Pursuing truth in thought and action, the mind attains a state of tranquillity and starts mirroring the truth of people, objects, events and situations well beyond constraints of time and space.

Build Up Your Immunity

Nimishananda Guru

We are blessed with an immune system that protects us from all sorts of infections and diseases. We maintain reasonably good health despite exposure to disease-causing agents because we have an in-built immune system and we maintain it with good eating and clean living habits. Just as we develop immunity in the body we need to develop immunity of the spirit to protect the purity of our heart, mind and soul and stay free of negativity.

Some of us are aware that we are exposed and susceptible to millions of negative vibrations from the external world, and to negativity in us. We need to transform ourselves from within to overcome negative karmas and influences. Negativities are an insult to the soul. They block the very light of the soul. Mind is a gift from God and we should not allow it to get polluted. In order to increase spiritual immunity, let's learn to overcome jealousy, doubt and unnecessary desires.

Another most common tendency is that we keep remembering and reliving the past, both achievements and traumas. We blame others for our misfortunes and take credit for our successes. But often we are responsible for our misfortunes, and we come to fear the future. Stop thinking of past achievements and failures and learn to live in the present. Then only we can come back to the original state of purity and build immunity of spirit.

When the ignorant irk us, we need to be patient and not get upset or retort. At the same time, we must acknowledge and accept the knowledge in others without being contemptuous or arrogant. Thus, when we calmly hear without reacting, we become immune to people's criticisms and praise that are meant to cloud our perspective. Then their negativity will not rub on us and we will be able to shore up good karma.

The young are impressionable and eager to learn. They are able to absorb divine vibrations easily, though they tend to be hot-headed and impatient. This could be why swearing comes so easily to them with a short temper and the desire to see instant results. This spoils the purity of their mind and heart. When purity and innocence is lost, grace stops flowing and you begin to accumulate bad karma! The older generation needs to come out of their comfort zone and the youth must come out of their impatient and adamant zone. We must be willing to identify and firmly resolve to drop off all our negative traits one by one right from young age itself so that the process of cultivating immunity begins.

Although the physical body is always impure, the mind should be kept clean. This will help us refine our intuitive powers so that we are able to decide what to do, when to do and how to do. Only when we are willing to learn do we begin to recognise, receive, retain and contain the Divinity in us.

Spiritual immunity protects us like a fortress from negative people, negative vibrations and karmic blocks from our past and present lives. It draws the best things to us. It fortifies and reinforces us with emotional and mental stability and builds up self-confidence. It makes us feel secure and in control. Due to spiritual immunity our innate powers are awakened and activated. We not only realize but also actualize that we are born as a light to illuminate.

No Fear of Dying

Bhagavan Shree Prasannaji

Death is powerless before the person who has depth of feeling for life. I have come across people who are not afraid of death, and they are from different walks of life. They include those in public life, householders and also convicted criminals. They seem to be ready for the ultimate act without feeling any remorse. But can we say that death is powerless before them and that they have depth in them as evidence of this? Perhaps not. Perhaps they are being seen as the strongest of people who have depth of knowledge that enables them to encounter death without fear.

It is very easy to end life or to say life ends you, regardless of your likes and dislikes. Every one of us on earth has to accept this fact and be prepared to leave the body at a given point of time. But where does death come into the picture if everyone is leaving the body lovingly and without fear? Can we live life with the trauma of the other who is dying? Can we live life without the fear of death haunting us? Can we live life with utmost freedom and happiness without being negative about living? Can we live life with full knowledge of life and its workings? Without knowing life we can never challenge death and make it feel its powerlessness.

You can never ever know life without being with death and feeling it first-hand. Death can never ever be logically explained as you have to know death to explain it. You have to die to know death...but you cannot explain without being alive. The nearest that you can get to death is to be with the dying and experience the trauma or otherwise, so as to feel the experience as best as possible, without actually dying — and this might help increase your depth of knowledge of death. Once you understand death and are ready to live with it life nourishes you so that you feel life to the fullest which in itself increases your depth of life.

Only when you feel death can you feel life, which opens the sublime qualities of intelligence, fearlessness, wisdom, love, happiness, joy, creativity, expression, truthfulness and life itself. If any of these is lacking in you then you cannot feel depth of yourself. You will be floating in life waiting for the tides to take you over and leave you on the shore. But the shore never appears unless you dive deep inside yourself without waiting for anyone's help to reach within. You have to overcome all the hurdles of negativities which hinder you in the form of greed, fear, attachment, dependency, ignorance and of course death, to reach your Self. You don't need to prove your depth to the other but certainly need to question yourself about what you know and be comfortable with the answer. You will find the true answer only in silence. And true silence can be felt only when all answers lose their depth.

No one in the world can reveal the secret for you but the secret reveals itself once you are ready to know it. You are the only one who can challenge yourself to know whether you have depth in you to know death.

Look at the Bright Side

Bhava Ram

 as this ever happened to you? Your life seems stressful, your task list is growing, work is dreadful, your relationships are a challenge, and you are angry and dissatisfied. Then you get a wicked cold. As it hits you with its full force, you look back to those terrible times you were experiencing just days earlier and they don't seem so bad. All you want now is for the cold to go away. Just feeling 'normal' would be a blessing — even with all of the frustrations that seemed to overwhelm you.

Singer Joni Mitchell memorialized this shifting mental process in 1970, with the song 'Big Yellow Taxi'. She bemoaned the destruction of nature, paradise being paved over for parking lots and the loss of relationship. The essence of her insight was embodied in the verse:

"Don't it always seem to go

That you don't know what you've got till it's gone?"

We take blessings for granted, as if they were our birthright, and we fixate on things that aggravate us. We miss out on much of the joy of daily life, unaware that our aggravation is a choice and that it arises from illusion.

"What do you mean," some might exclaim indignantly, "my overbearing boss is neither my choice nor an illusion." But our reaction to the situation is our choice. We can choose to loathe our boss, complain to our colleagues, and wallow in self-pity. What would be the result? More stress, unhappiness and lack of vocational fulfilment. Or we could choose to use the situation for personal advancement. We can seek options, such as entering into dialogue with our boss to find common ground, or find a new job or focus on aspects of work that we find rewarding. Take skilful action.

The world is never what our ego and self-centredness demands that it be. Not everyone will see the greatness we see in ourselves or constantly seek to affirm us. Our reactions to situations that don't fit our illusion cause us to suffer. If we were fired from that miserable job we might shift perspectives unconsciously and begin to mourn our loss, suddenly realizing how fond we were of our colleagues, how rewarding much of the work was, and we might even recall times when our boss gave us praise. Once again, by choice, we would be suffering. "Don't it always seem to go....?"

You might be able to review your life and see ways in which your choice of reactions to life has only increased your pain. You might also notice that much of the negative self-talk in our busy minds is based upon reactions to a reality that does not conform to our illusory expectations. It's even likely that we are not seeing the full reality, but instead viewing it through the constricted prism of our smaller self, or ego...

Make a list of your blessings right now. Friends, freedom, material abundance, mobility, yoga classes, recreational activities, books, spiritual pursuits and more. Everything is a blessing because it is the most profound of blessings just to be here. Just to experience the miracle of being.

With a constant sense of gratitude come peace, contentment and the unfolding of a whole new world before our eyes...a world in which we live in awe of life. To cultivate gratitude, I invite you to say 'thank you' to everyone and everything. For, all too soon, our time shall pass.

A Triumph of Spirit

Ami Patel

eciding to skip a dinner invitation last Saturday night I settled down to watch the 30th year celebrations of the Art of Living that were being telecast live from Berlin. As the programme began I stared at the TV screen, thinking: Are those water droplets on the camera? "Please God, let it not be rain," I pleaded in prayer. "We have been waiting for this wonderful event for months; how can it rain!"

The evening had begun with a beautiful Sanskrit rendition by Grammy award winner Chandrika Tandon and her team. I watched, spellbound, as they continued to perform smilingly, completely oblivious to the rain that was gaining momentum. And it looked so windy, too. The ensemble included Swiss Alpine horns with 2,000 Bulgarian dancers in flower-petal formation, looking beautiful from an aerial view. An aboriginal dance for mother earth, 2,000 guitarists making music, and 300 pianists under transparent canopies — all seemed to not mind the rain in the least.

An international community of hundreds of yogis demonstrated Suryanamaskars and yogasanas to the chant of Sanskrit *shlokas*. Here 1 was, on a muggy day in Mumbai, glued to the TV while some 50,000 seekers and masters were enjoying themselves thoroughly despite the cold, wet weather in Berlin that day. "I wish you could take a flight and come here right now," SMS-ed my friend Mala, who was in the midst of it all.

"I have no words to describe what it's like to be here," she added.

"Aren't you freezing," I asked.

"Who cares," she said, as she waited patiently for peace meditation to begin. This is a triumph of spirit, a spirit that rain cannot dampen, that the cold cannot freeze — the same spirit that even bad times cannot touch. This is the spirit that rose and soared, revealing itself in its full glory that day. Guruji (Sri Sri Ravi Shankar) said in Berlin: "When we started planning this event, we decided that the theme song would be 'rainbow colours' — and the rains have come!

We seem to have invited the rain gods."

I went back to three years ago in New York City where I was to style a special fashion shoot, all the way from Central Park to Times Square down to Soho. Every location was carefully examined and planned. Except for the weather, of course that was not in our control. The warm, bright summer day turned into a rainy, stormy day with heavy downpours and claps of thunder — just when I was to begin the shoot, as luck would have it.

"Let's do the entire shoot at the place called Dumbo under the Brooklyn Bridge!"

The photographer was trying to salvage the situation.

What, is this why I put in all this effort and came this long way?

"Let's shoot in the rain," I said, holding an umbrella over him and his expensive camera.

"You shoot at a slow shutter speed and let's see what happens."

The result was spectacular; the result was models sashaying against the rain-textured New York City skyline — it was almost like a soft painting. Needless to say, it was much talked about for months to come.

I read this in the Yoga Vasistha: "Adversity can be prosperity and prosperity can truly be adversity depending on how you look at it."

In death you have no choice, but if you consciously allow the spirit to triumph in every phase of your life, then that is called the Art of Living!

Renounce Wealth to Enjoy it

Osho

he Ishavasya Upanishad says your ego will disappear if you cease to call anything yours. "Everything in the universe is controlled and owned by the Lord. Accept only those things that are necessary..."

Don't entertain a desire for anybody's wealth. Why? When nothing can be mine, then neither can anything be yours. Be aware, because the *sutra,* "Don't covet; don't desire another's riches," has been greatly misinterpreted.

Most commentators have explained it thus: "It is a sin to desire another's wealth, so don't entertain such a desire." But the first part of the *sutra* says that wealth belongs to nobody; it is existence's. "When it is not mine, how can it be yours?"

Its true meaning is this — do not wish for another's wealth because the wealth which is not mine is also not yours. So desire has no grounds on which to stand. No expert of ethics can get at the real meaning of this *sutra.* It is subtle and deep. The moralist is anxious to see that no one steals another's property; no one should consider as his own what belongs to another. But his emphasis on another's property is just the converse side of his emphasis on what is his own. Remember, the person who says, "This is yours," is not free from the notion, "This is mine," because these two are different sides of the same coin. As long as the feeling persists, "The building is mine," its counterpart, "The building is yours," will continue.

So don't wish for another's property, because it belongs to no one. I don't mean simply that it is sinful to seize another's property with a view to making it your own. It is a sin in the first place to consider it either his or yours. It is a sin to look upon it as anybody's or to pretend ownership is anyone's but existence's. If you can comprehend this interpretation, then and only then will you be able to grasp the deep and subtle meaning of the Ishavasya.

Otherwise the apparent meaning of these *sutras* is that each should securely possess his own property and, to protect his own interests, should propagate on all sides that no one should wish for another's property. So stealing and extorting is useless, meaningless and irrelevant. There is no skill or art in it. It is as good as labour lost. It is trying to draw a line on water.

Enjoy wealth by renouncing it. It is said that if you renounce a thing, you can enjoy it. The statement is very antithetical to our belief. They alone become real masters who refuse to be masters. Everything falls into the hands of those who have no desire to hold onto things.

People have misinterpreted these *sutras*. "Enjoy through renunciation" has come to mean that if you give in charity, you will be rewarded with heaven. But pay attention: the *sutra* says, "He who renounces, receives." It does not say, "He who gives up with a view to getting, will receive." In fact, he who gives up with a view to getting does not give up, because he is just working out how to get the reward. This *sutra* makes a straight, simple statement that he who renounces, enjoys. It does not say, "Give up if you desire to enjoy." It announces that if you can give up, then you can enjoy; but if you are nursing the idea of enjoyment, you can never renounce.

The Third Eye of Wisdom

Baskaran Pillai

nce, the Tamil saint Manikkavasagar, who was the chief minister of a Pandiyan king, was sent on a mission to buy horses for the military. On the way, he met Shiva who appeared in human form, as a guru. Shiva simply looked at Manikkavasagar and the latter got completely transformed. Manikkavasagar forgot all about his identity as chief minister, about his wife and children — all these identities vanished into thin air. He used the money that the king had given him to buy horses, to build a temple for Shiva. After the initiation was over, Shiva disappeared. Manikkavasagar recounted that during this meeting he had a trade-off with Shiva:

"You give your Self to me and take my 'self'."

He wondered who had the better trade-off; while Shiva got nothing from him, Manikkavasagar received everything. Hence it is said that a true guru is the one who can give you liberation just by a glance.

The Shiva Sutras mention a path called 'Shambava Upaya', which refers to receiving the results of meditation instantaneously. Here, you experience an immediate expansion in your awareness and acquire divine consciousness. Actually, it is not accomplished through meditation; it is done through the grace of the guru. You don't do anything; you don't even meditate, once you have a guru in your life. Through grace, the guru is able to transfer everything to you.

You can read books and gain understanding about the process of enlightenment. However, you will still remain in the theoretical domain. The fundamental thing in enlightenment is the opening of the third eye. The third eye will just not open by theoretical understanding and it is extremely rare to open it through one's own practice. You need to do more than that. When the third eye opens, you can always stay in a higher state of consciousness and are totally focused on God. Then, you are not pulled by karma, *maya* and ego, and do not return to the old state of consciousness. Then, you know what is going to happen in the future and what is going to happen to the world. The third eye is also the place for manifesting your thoughts and desires.

How can you open the third eye? You can do that through grace. Keep on praying for mercy. When the divine light enters the third eye, you will find that you are awakened. Who is going to do that? It is the guru. That's why, in Indic spiritual tradition, the guru is considered everything. What about the traditions and religions where there is no guru? There, the Messiah and the Prophet are gurus. They are called by different names; they are representatives of God on earth. In karma removal too, the guru can play a great role. When you open your mind and spirit to the guru, it can help you to remove your ego, the part within you which holds on to karmic thoughts and actions.

Why do we focus on the guru's feet? It is to cultivate humility, to banish the ego. Keep visualizing the feet of the guru; surrender to his wisdom and learn to acquire knowledge. By doing so, you can teach yourself to completely overcome suffering and doubt. The guru's feet will help access divine energy and bring you incredible peace. You will be transformed.

Love for Love's Sake

Sudhamahi Regunathan

age Yagyavalkya was in an assembly where many philosophers had gathered. He was being bombarded with questions. Among the questioners were Gargi and her 18-year-old niece, Maitreyi. As Maitreyi watched Yagyavalkya demolish every philosopher's misconception and answer every question with erudition and wisdom, she fell in love with him. Maitreyi, who was Gargi's brother Mitra's daughter, was already sensitive to and interested in philosophical discourse as she grew up hearing philosophy from her aunt. Now having heard and seen Yagyavalkya, the young girl wished to learn from him.

However, there was a problem: How could she learn from a man? Would that not set tongues wagging? Worse, she found Yagyavalkya was already married and that too to a wonderful lady called Katyayani. Maitreyi confided in her aunt and her parents and eventually the celebrated aunt and father reached Yagyavalkya's doorstep to tell him of Maitreyi's resolve.

Yagyavalkya said his body already belonged to another and he could not answer or accede to their request. They then approached Katyayani and she consented. Maitreyi lived a happy life, learning all wisdom from her husband. Then one day Yagyavalkya decided he would renounce the world and become an ascetic. He divided his property into two parts; he was not worried about Katyayani — she would accept his decision and her share and live happily. The problem came with Maitreyi. Would she accept?

As Yagyavalkya had feared, Maitreyi did not accept his decision. She asked him if his wealth would get her immortality. No, said her husband. "Nothing can buy immortality." In another discussion he had likened the tree to man and said while a tree regenerates even after being cut, man does not appear to do so. It is the soul, the Brahmn or *atman* that is born again. This he explains with different examples to Maitreyi. "But," asks Maitreyi, "when the visible world disappears, how does Brahmn remain?"

Yagyavalkya gives the example of a grain of salt, which is the same from within and without and dissolves without any sign in water. That he says is how the Brahmn functions. Salt has the same taste — as a solid and after it is immersed in any liquid. Such is Brahmn, the all-pervasive oneness.

Yagyavalkya, however, recognizes that to appreciate that everything is Brahmn, one ought to first develop detachment from the world. Or else how does one view it objectively? So he begins by saying that the love for the husband or the son or for anything for that matter is not for them but more for one's own sake. "We are husband and wife Maitreyi; why do you love me? Do you love me for my sake? I don't think so. Something within you draws satisfaction through your love for me. That something in you is the soul. Because your own *atman* is dear to you, caused by contact with that *atman*, objects considered as your own also become dear. However, the *atman* itself is entirely free from all relationships."

We love mainly for the satisfaction and comfort it gives us. We love because we want to love. To realize this truth is to realize the importance of the people around you. They give you some satisfaction; you need to love them. So one can draw comfort from the fact that even the attachment for the other is rooted in the beauty of one's own soul...and in that beauty every soul is one.

To Succeed, You Need Concentration

Swami Kriyananda

n every level of mental activity, concentration is the key to success. The student is taking an exam but is distracted by a popular song running through his head. The businessman trying to write an important contract is worried over an argument he'd had with his wife. The judge is distracted by a teenager appearing before him as he resembles his own son. Lack of concentration means inefficiency. But what is not generally known is that a concentrated mind succeeds not only because it can solve problems with greater dispatch, but also because problems have a way of somehow vanishing before its focused energies, without even requiring to be solved.

A concentrated mind often attracts opportunities for success that, to less focused (and therefore less successful) individuals, appear to come by sheer luck. The one who concentrates receives inspiration and this may often be thought of as a divine favour by others. But such seeming 'favours' are due simply to the power of concentration.

Concentration awakens our powers and channels them, dissolving obstacles in our path, attracting opportunities, insights, and inspirations. In many ways, concentration is the single most important key to success. This is particularly true in yoga practice. The mind, in meditation, must be so perfectly still that not a ripple of thought enters it. God, the subtlest reality, cannot be perceived except in utter silence. Much of the teaching of yoga, therefore, centres on techniques designed especially for developing concentration.

Ask, what is concentration? Concentration implies, first, an ability to release one's mental and emotional energies from all other interests and involvements and, second, an ability to focus them on a single object or state of awareness. Concentration may assume various manifestations, from a dynamic outpouring of energy, to perfectly quiescent perceptions. In its higher stages, concentration becomes so deep that there is no longer any question of its remaining merely a practice: The yogi becomes so completely identified with the object of his concentration that he and it, as well as the act of concentration itself, become one. In this way, he can gain a far deeper understanding of it than would be possible by aloof scientific objectivity alone.

In concentration on our own higher realities, identification with them becomes lasting. For in this case there is no other, more personal, reality to come back to. We are those realities. We are the infinite light, and love, and joy, and wisdom of God.

The most effective technique of concentration will therefore be one which both interiorizes the mind and permits a gradual transition from technical practice to utter stillness. In that state, the senses become automatically stilled, permitting an undisturbed continuation of the concentrated state. Once the mind is so perfectly focused, its concentrated power may be applied to any object one wishes.

The techniques of concentration are like finger exercises on the piano, which enable one to play fluently but are no substitute for actual playing. Once your mind has become focused and quiet, it is time to forego the practice of techniques, and offer your entire awareness calmly up to God. Concentration leads naturally to that state in which the will, no longer busily engaged in outward planning, can be uplifted in a pure act of becoming. Concentration, directed in this way, becomes ecstasy.

Living in Constant Fear

Deepak M Ranade

ear remains deeply entrenched within us; it is one of the most primitive of emotions that ensures self-preservation. This emotion is mediated by the limbic system, which is phylogenetically the oldest of the nervous systems. It is an integral third of the 'fight, fright and flight' response. Fear as a physiological reaction has a definite evolutionary role, but when it outgrows this primal scope and becomes pathological, it can wreak havoc. Fear plays an integral role in determining the happiness quotient of life.

The index of equanimity is guided by the degree of the fear of the unknown. It can drive a person to paranoia if he is a control freak or redeem him totally if he surrenders to the unknown. Fear is in the future, never in the present. Eventually, today becomes the tomorrow that we feared yesterday.

There is a primordial form of fear that keeps one always on the edge. It is 'existential angst'. It is characterized by a sense of constant persecution, a fear of a grand conspiracy and a sense of impending doom. This psychological anxiety, sooner than later, manifests itself as a plethora of somatic ailments.

The following story is illustrative: There was once a little mouse that lived in constant fear of the cat. The anxiety of running into the cat made it live a life of misery. God, overcome with sympathy, decided to turn the mouse into a cat so as to allay its fears. No sooner did this happen than the cat began to get nightmares about the dog. Wanting to appease the tortured soul, God turned the cat into a dog. However, the newly created dog now began to get fearful thoughts about being chased by the tiger. The Omniscient One understands even without words, and soon enough, the dog was converted into a tiger. Becoming a tiger should have been the end of all his woes, but no, this 'tiger' felt the creeps at the thought of an armed hunter, who might spot him and then... At this point, God turned the tiger back into a mouse. He said to the mouse, "No physical form will ever rid you of your fear, because the fear is not of your form. It is in your imagination, and that unfortunately is not in my control."

On closer examination it is evident that fear stems from resentment and anxiety about imminent unpleasant events... Despite the knowledge of one's helplessness in shaping the turn of future events, fear stems from the imaginary "What if?" It is common knowledge that anxiety about an unpleasant event is worse than actually dealing with the event itself. This is because the imagination conjures all sorts of potential 'worse than' scenarios. The actual event very often passes off as an anti-climax. Thus fear tends to magnify only the negative outcomes. A positive attitude in such situations leans more on 'better than' scenarios. Both schools of thought don't change reality. They only modulate the mindset by making it either bearable or unbearable.

If fear were to be viewed merely as a biological construct, just an instinct for survival, then the tiny mouse would be as fearless as the hunter without physically having to transform into one.

It's all About Your Attitude

Sreeram Manoj Kumar

The main cause of bondage is identifying Self with body and mind, both of which are not eternal. The body is constantly changing. We assume doership through the mind — which we identify as our Self — and any action performed by thought, word and deed is wrongly associated with Self. But the Self is non-doer; it is just a witness. Only the ignorant consider the Self as doer. A person who is aware of this truth is free from bondage of the subtle body which is the mind and intellect concept. Such a person is able to evolve to higher realms.

The sentence "I am not the doer, Providence alone is the doer" means that my wisdom and the thinking capacity that is in me would not have been possible if the One present in all of us is not guiding my thoughts. I am not the actor, writer or performer — someone is acting, writing or performing through me; that One is the Cosmic Self, whatever name we might wish to assign to the Power.

It is the knowledge of a *jnani* or the emotional feeling of a *bhakta* that brings out non-doership which annihilates ego. An unchecked ego hinders the flow of thoughts. Tons of praise may come your way from those who appreciate creative work produced by your efforts. And the praise may sometimes make you feel proud. Yet it makes sense to let all the praise reach the One who is guiding you, so that there is no hindrance for further flow of thoughts.

You don't have to imbibe non-doership; it should be as naturally present as hunger is present. Does a lion need to learn how to hunt? Or a deer, how to flee? No, it is just there as a natural instinct. Similarly, having the skill to understand non-doership should come naturally to the one who has become the *drashta* or seer; or perhaps who is just a witness. Only the ignorant would say that every event is happening due to them.

For *karya* or something to happen, three things are necessary: *karana* or the person who does the job, parent material and the instrument to do it. Take, for instance, the making of a pot. You have the potter who makes the pot, the parent material clay and the instrument to make the pot — the potter's wheel. If the pot (*karya*) has to be made, the potter will use clay and the potter's wheel. Here the potter is *abhinna karana* or undifferentiated cause, clay is *upadana karana* or essential cause while the potter's wheel is *nimitta karana* or the instrumental cause. Hence the potter's wheel cannot take credit for the pot. The credit goes to the potter and clay. A potter can choose any potter's wheel he wishes. Similarly, in our lives we are all like the potter's wheel in the hands of the great Potter, the Supreme. Neither are we potter or clay; the Supreme is all three.

What is so special in having an attitude of non-doership? At the gross level it will keep ego in check. At the subtle level, it will not let you become the *bhokta,* the enjoyer. I am neither *karta* nor *bhokta.* This will ensure that one does not return in another life to enjoy or suffer the fruits of past deeds. The attitude of non-doership would put an end to the cycle of birth and death.

Shower all with Blessings

Mohanji

lessing expands you. It makes you light. When we bless all the people — those whom we like and those whom we dislike — we become the perfect expression of the Almighty. His true expression is unconditional love. When we remove all hatred and fear from our minds, we become embodiments of love.

Love expands. Love makes our life enjoyable. When we express sincere gratitude to all objects and beings that enable our existence on earth, we become universal. Once we understand the true relevance of the food that we have consumed so far, the houses that sheltered us, the books that gave us knowledge, our parents and teachers and, above all, the Divinity that sustained us, we will be filled with humility and deep gratitude.

Most of our vital functions including respiration, circulation, digestion, heartbeat and even sleep for that matter, are controlled by our subconscious mind. All these things are working in perfect synchronization because our conscious mind has nothing to do with it. We are given time, space, intellect and situation to give expression to our inherent traits.

No single person is in control of everything. There is no sense in blaming any one person when something goes wrong or to entertain feelings of guilt. What is there to be afraid of? All experiences have been lessons. We could not have changed anything. So, there is little else to do than express unconditional love and compassion. We might as well bless everybody and everything. When we realize that we are not really the one who does everything, we will see our ego getting nullified and our doer-ship getting dissolved. We will then operate in perfect awareness and gratitude.

God (who is in us) is to be loved, not feared. The soul element that fuels our existence is the God within us — Generator, Operator and Destroyer. All of us have the same God element. None is inferior or superior to anyone else. Some have evolved to higher realms through rigorous practices, contemplation and meditation. Through lifetimes of efforts, they attained higher awareness. That's all. In principle, all are one and the same.

All of us are temporary custodians of body and all our possessions. It is the same with relationships too. Everything is temporary. Everything has a definite lifespan. Once we accept this truth, there is no room for egocentric expressions. All we can do is to forgive everything. Bless everything.

When we shift our consciousness to the spine — and to 360 degrees — the impact and wear and tear of events around us will be very little. Nothing will touch us deeply. Nothing will overwhelm us. You will maintain perfect equanimity and deep gratitude. Nothing happens by accident. Everything has a perfect reason. We often cannot understand the reason from our level of consciousness. Our inability should not be interpreted as cosmic deficiency. Cosmic perfection is infinite and incomparable.

All of us exist in various planes of consciousness. We carry the conditionings of our immediate past as well as other lives without having clarity about it. We cannot usually figure out which conditioning provoked which response in us. But invariably we are victims of our conditionings. Hence, it is important to touch base with our own consciousness; our real Self. We are one family and one consciousness. We will never be separate from one another.

Conflict Necessary
for Creativity

Raj Kachroo

hen MK Gandhi was thrown out of a train in South Africa he had a choice to make — either to ignore the event and live in peace or enter into a conflict and face harassment, hardship and the possibility of getting physically hurt He chose the latter Why? Did he not have a guru who had taught him that living in peace and tranquillity was the ultimate objective of life and the best way to achieve this objective was to avoid situations of conflict? Why did he not walk away? The Dalai Lama chose to live in exile rather than live in peace in Tibet. He is a spiritual master himself. He preaches peace around the world. Does he not know that living in peace requires avoiding situations of conflict? Aung San Suu Kyi did not have to stay in jail. Winston Churchill did not have to join the World War. Nelson Mandela did not have to suffer in solitary confinement. Julius Nyerere did not have to fight a war with Idi Amin. There is a long list of people who have embraced conflict despite standing for peace, otherwise. They had the courage to stand up against repression rather than submit to it.

Both the *Ramayana* and the *Mahabharata*, revered Indic epics, are stories of war, not peace Krishna did not tell the Pandavas to ignore the incident of Draupadi's humiliation in court (the Draupadi *vastraharan*). He encouraged them to go to war. The *Bhagavad Gita* says engaging in war to uphold truth is not a matter of choice for a warrior; it is his duty. Islam says participation in *jihad* is the duty of a Muslim when the fight is to uphold justice when challenged by oppression, as a way of self-defence.

Most are confused between conflict and the method of resolving a conflict. We assume, incorrectly, that Gandhi, as a peace loving person, must have avoided situations of conflict. On the other hand, he faced conflict head-on. Bhagat Singh and Gandhi were both gearing themselves to deal with conflict, except that Gandhi tried to employ peaceful means while Bhagat Singh chose aggression. The duty of a scientist, artist or professor is also to engage in conflict against repressive regimes of knowledge.

Any kind of limited knowledge is a form of bondage. Albert Einstein advanced the boundaries of scientific knowledge. James Joyce did the same in the world of literature. He flouted rules of writing as he saw them as restrictions on creativity. Picasso and MF Husain for example, explored realms beyond accepted rules in visual art. Mother Teresa redefined the concept of caring. Every one of them faced criticism and controversy, yet they remained convinced of the nature of their work and the methods they used to fulfill their vision.

They remained engaged. One can only conclude from this that people we admire and even those whom we worship have all rejected the existing as being adequate and have chosen to engage in conflict to expand the existing. They have redefined the purpose of our life. The purpose of our life is not to live in passive acceptance but to engage with conflict in order to be creative. Creativity is the purpose of life. The purpose is to advance an individual soul and advance collective Consciousness. The only word of caution here is that we must first settle ourselves spiritually so that we know whether a conflict is justified or not.

Irritants can Teach You Lessons

Marguerite Theophil

When a particularly obnoxious person — according to you, that is — shows up prominently in your life, it's time to find your submerged sense of humour and say: "Oh, this must be Teacher of Life Lesson 579 for me!" Or 700, or whatever. Know that there are, and will be, many such teachers…

In many spiritual traditions, we are taught to see obstacles or trouble, especially in the form of people who bring in or represent them, as challenges for growing, for moving on. When a person repeatedly upsets, harms or otherwise does something negative towards you, you might think "This will end," or "He will change", and focus on other things. But often you notice that this just does not happen. Let's say a particularly annoying arrogant person, X, is a frequent part of your life. You avoid having much to do with this person. After a while X moves away, or changes jobs. You are relieved; no more contact with this painful person. The problem is no longer there; it no longer triggers your hostility or pain. But sooner or later, Y shows up. Just as arrogant, just as annoying. Same thing happens, triggering emotions which upset you — because nothing has been learned.

What X and Y are both oddly making very clear is that you have something here to work on; offering you an opportunity to know yourself better, and put into practice any specific approaches and skills you need in order to grow and evolve.

Now it's also very important to discern what exactly this lesson you are supposed to learn is. In this case, perhaps your particular lesson is to develop empathy, understand what makes X and Y behave this way. Or maybe it is something else altogether: to find the courage to be assertive, to speak up for your rights, to draw the line. A good rule of thumb, if you are confused, is to go for what seems harder for you.

For an impatient person, speaking up for yourself is easy; but pausing before jumping in and confronting, or reflecting on what made the other person angry — that is far more difficult. For a person with not enough courage, it is easier to 'forgive and forget' or make excuses for the other person's behaviour than to say a firm 'No', or be brave enough to disagree, or speak up about one's distress.

Your 'teacher', in this way, pushes you to move out of your particular comfort zone, to change and grow more whole. Your teacher also serves another function — to act as a kind of mirror of your own behaviour or approaches that might need to change. A good indicator is the negative labels you place on others. If you grumble about an 'unreasonable' person, or several of them, perhaps you are being unreasonable somewhere. If you meet someone you find is extremely 'thoughtless', stop and reflect: is there somebody you are being thoughtless towards too? If too many 'stubborn' people show up — you know what to check up on!

This is not comfortable. I am currently struggling with someone I see as a person who 'takes others for granted'. So I can decide to learn both kinds of lessons. I can choose to give it time, but not to let it slide; to discuss it with her politely, but firmly. And as I reflect, I can also realize and admit that to some extent in my life, I am doing the same thing to others.

Towards Freedom from Corruption

Sri Sri Ravi Shankar

rom being perceived as a country of snake charmers to becoming a hub of IT and rediscovered spirituality, the image of India has had a makeover in recent years. Only the power of spirituality can help resolve the problems we face today. MK Gandhi used this power to help India secure independence. While India has been fortunate to have an entire generation that dedicated itself to the cause of freedom, there is another that has driven the country into the morass of corruption and crime.

We need people of character and honesty to check corruption. Corruption begins where a sense of belonging ends. Corruption is present at many levels of society; the first level is in the minds of the general public. We tell God that if you do this work of mine then I will offer something to you. Let alone our bosses, we don't even spare God. Secondly, there are bribe givers and takers at the official level. The third level of corruption is at the ministerial level.

Lack of faith, belongingness, human values, sacrifice and service attitude are all causes of corruption, as also selfish motives and a sense of insecurity. It is when you feel so insecure and think that money is the only power or strength, then you become corrupt to the core. There is a lack of role models and inspiring examples at the highest levels. Also lack of stringent laws and effective enforcement of existing laws engender corruption at all levels.

Corruption starts where belongingness ends. Nobody will ever ask for a bribe from his family and dear ones. The means through which we can spread belongingness is spirituality. Work hard, be self-sufficient and stand on your own feet. We have to instil the belief that whatever is yours, you will get. Inner strength and awareness needs to be awakened. Only then, constructive change is possible. The younger generation has to resolve to save the country and its people from corruption and crime. They have to take responsibility on their own and strive for sustainable development and realize that they have a huge potential and strength to achieve whatever they want. The youth need to believe that it is possible to be creative and productive without losing the humanness that is intrinsic in us. Spirituality kindles, sustains and enhances enthusiasm and enthusiasm is what drives us towards achieving our goals.

We need to see ourselves as universal people to attain a holistic personality, where there is appreciation for all ways of life and culture. We could learn the right things from everyone — be it teamwork from the Japanese, precision from the Germans, decency from the British and marketing skills from the Americans. And above all, human values from our rich tradition and spiritual heritage.

With one-sixth of the world's population, India now needs to take its rightful place on the world stage. We need to become more confident and take more pride in our cultural and spiritual roots; to harness spiritual values to fight terrorism and other social evils. Inter-faith harmony on the basis of an all-inclusive spiritual movement is needed to prevent young minds from turning to violence.

The government must focus more on 'gross domestic happiness' rather than 'gross domestic product'. Prosperity has meaning when there is happiness and common welfare built into the system. Let's work towards building a corruption-free society by cultivating a spiritual outlook that helps us evolve on the right path.

Freedom & Responsibility

Osho

 esponsibility and freedom go together. If you don't want to take responsibility, you can't have freedom either. The two come together or they go together. If you shun responsibility, you have to accept slavery in some way or other.

Now, you had dreamed about freedom without ever thinking that great responsibility will follow. Freedom you have, but you have not fulfilled the responsibility. Hence, sadness lingers around you. You are absolutely capable of removing this sadness. If you were capable of destroying your slavery, your chains, you are certainly capable of being creative. Freedom means you will have to be responsible for every act, for every breath; whatever you do or don't do, you will be responsible.

People are really in deep fear of freedom, although they talk about freedom. But my own experience is: very few people really want freedom; because they are subconsciously aware that freedom will bring many problems that they are not ready to face. It is better to remain in cozy imprisonment. It is warmer, and what will you do with freedom? Unless you are ready to be a seeker, a searcher, a creator...Very few people want to go on a pilgrimage or to go into deeper silences of the heart, or to take the responsibility of love. The implications are great.

You will have to dispel that darkness, otherwise sooner or later you will enter into a prison. You cannot go on burdening yourself with sadness. Before the burden becomes too much and forces you back into slavery, into imprisonment, change the whole situation by being a creative person. Just find out what is your joy in life, what you would like to create, what you would like to be, what you want to be your definition.

Freedom is simply an opportunity to find a definition for yourself, a true, authentic individuality, and a joy in making the world around you a little better, a little more beautiful — a few more roses, a little more greenery and a few more oases.

Madame Blavatsky, founder of the Theosophical Society, used to carry two bags in her hands, always. Either going for a morning walk or travelling in a train — those two bags were always in her hands. And she was throwing something out of those bags — from the window while sitting in the train — onto the side of the train.

People would ask, "Why do you do this?"

She would say, "This has been my whole life's habit. These are seasonal flower seeds. I may not come back on this route again, but that does not matter. When the season comes and the flowers will blossom, thousands of people who pass every day in this line of railway trains will see those flowers, those colours. They will not know me. That does not matter.

"One thing is certain: I am making a few people happy somewhere. That much I know. It does not matter whether they know it or not. What matters is that I have been doing something which will make somebody happy. Some children may come and pluck a few flowers and go home. Some lovers may come and make garlands for each other. And without their knowing, I will be part of their love. And I will be part of the joy of children. And I will be part of those who will be simply passing by the path, seeing the beautiful flowers."

Satyagraha to Fight Injustice

E Sudhakar

he concept of satyagraha is related to the social, political, cultural, economic and psychological conditions which influenced the life and personality of MK Gandhi. He adopted the non-violent approach to resist all the forces that exerted pressure on him physically and psychologically. He believed that the supreme law that governs all living things and the universe is nothing but love and non-violence. It was Gandhi's firm belief that the basis of all religions of the world was the law of love. The very purpose of non-violent resistance and upholding the principles of truth was none other than asserting the freedom of oneself over his mind and body.

Gandhi's concept of Satyagraha is an integrated concept and includes truth, non-violence, non-stealing, chastity or *brahmacharya*, poverty or non-possession, bread labour, fearlessness, control of the palate (*asvada*), tolerance, *swadeshi* and removal of untouchability. According to Gandhi, satyagraha can be adopted by anybody. He said that satyagraha was like a Banyan tree which had innumerable branches. *Satya* and *ahimsa* together made its parent trunk from which all the innumerable branches shoot out. Satyagraha has also been considered as a weapon of soul force to resist any kind of oppression.

While Gandhi regarded satyagraha as a way of life, during the freedom struggle of India, satyagraha was used as a weapon to resist the authority of the state and to achieve public welfare. Satyagraha as a means of resistance and conflict resolution has different forms. Hunger strike or fasting, *hartal* or striking work and *hijrat* or immigration are some of the forms suggested. The principles, conditions and qualifications of satyagraha are relevant to all these forms.

Is satyagraha relevant today? There is no simple 'yes' or 'no' answer to this question. When we try to decide whether it is relevant to the present day society, the fundamental thing we have to consider is the nature of the present-day individual. Gandhi was well aware of the increasing influence of materialistic considerations on the modern society and individual. According to him, the main objective of satyagraha was to reform the opponent. In the present socio-economic political system, there is a need to wean the individual away from the influence of wealth, luxuries and power. In all educational institutions, right from the lowest level to the level of university, it would be worthwhile to teach young people the concept of satyagraha and the principles of truth and non-violence, as the basic factors contributing to the peace, harmony and welfare of society.

In industrial establishments and other places of mass employment, satyagraha would be a viable alternative to other methods for the peaceful resolution of disputes and conflicts. In all walks of life, wherever there is scope for conflict and disharmony, the practice of the principles of truth and non-violence in the smallest way possible, would definitely make a great contribution in bringing about peace and harmony. Satyagraha as an ideal and as a great weapon of conflict resolution will always serve as inspiration to people of all generations to come, worldwide. Without truth and non-violence, there cannot be peace and without peace there cannot be development.

Connecting to Your Guru

Nayaswami Kriyananda

We are living in a time of great change. We need to turn to spirituality for direction. A true guru could be of great help here. Too often, however, you find that people who are trying to attune themselves to the guidance of saints are actually just tuning into their personalities. My guru, Paramahansa Yogananda, had a wonderful personality — strong, yet sweet, loving, and supportive. It was easy to tune oneself to that level of his being.

I didn't really court an outward contact with my guru, although he gave me a lot of personal time, told many stories, and gave many instructions in private. The most important thing was the inner contact. When there was a group around him, I would always want to be at the back, so that I could just feel his vibrations.

To have true contact with the guru you need to establish contact inside. This is what is important and meaningful, because it's where you have your true relationship with the guru. So, if you have a guru or wish to have one, when you try to attune with him, don't think in terms of his personality, beautiful though it may be. Try to go deeper and contact his spirit. Touch him at his centre, in his cosmic nature. This, too, is where we originate, where our own being, as a separate soul, gets its beginnings. We are that, from time immemorial. This is why a saint with sufficient spiritual development can recognize you, even after not having had contact with you for many lives. Your body and your personality may have changed, but your essence never changes. That is the reality you want to try to touch in your teacher.

To feel that inner core, meditate on your guru. This is the real master, the real guru. From that consciousness, he will be able to guide and enliven you. It's not that he imposes his reality on yours, but rather that he is able to animate your own reality. He comes from within, like a light that shines and illuminates your understanding and changes every aspect of your life.

It's good to pray for help, for guidance — not only good, but necessary. But, most of all, ask him to give you greater consciousness of your own Self, and of your devotion to the Infinite. Get to your core. We were born in eternity, and we have gone through many millions of lives. It takes a long time to understand who we truly are. But in all of this, there's been a germ of longing. Deeply we ask, "Where will I find love? Where will I find the joy that I'm looking for? Where will I find the fulfilment that my soul wants?"

This longing for love, for fulfilment, for joy, and for understanding is the central core of your being. You have your own way of wanting it. You have your own way of going out to find it, but that's who you are. Nothing else. This longing has come from the infinite — from the ever-existing, ever-conscious, ever-new joy — and that longing can never be satisfied until you once again go back to that. This is who the guru is. Get to know him on that level, and the longing of countless incarnations will be fulfilled forever in that infinite consciousness.

Life & Death: An Enigma

Swami Sukhabodhananda

hat happens to our soul when we die? If one dies unfulfilled, what happens to the soul? The physical or gross body is called sthulashariram. Our limited self, the subtle body, is called sukshmashariram. Sthulashariram is the abode of *jivatma,* the spirit of life. It is not the body, but it gets identified with the body. The soul, along with the mind, is the seat of consciousness. The body is only a vehicle, and when it is consigned to flames after physical death, the soul is set free. Then it searches for another body that will be its vehicle for another lifetime. At the end of this search, depending upon its karma in life till then, it is assigned to a particular body. The soul begins life anew in that body. In reality, the soul is immortal.

The space in a room appears limited by the room. Is the space enclosed within the four walls of the room or is the room a small enclosure in the vast unlimited space in the universe? The room is a tiny speck in space. But we say there is space in the room. Think of the *jivatma* as space and of the body as the walls of the room that encloses part of the space. If the walls of the room crumble, will the space previously contained here suffer any damage or dissolution? No, the space returns to its state of continuity which it had earlier with the space outside the walls. Once we realize this, we know that physical death means the release of our immortal soul from the confines of our mortal body. This realization is *gnanodayam,* the dawn of knowledge.

Doesn't the cycle of birth, death and rebirth negate the law of karma? No, it means that the soul is on an unending journey of evolution. The question is whether you want to hasten this process, or you want to allow this process to happen at its own pace. For example, if you are into agriculture, you pump water into your fields when there is no rain for a long period. The water accelerates crop growth which would otherwise be slowed down by delayed rains. Irrigation technology speeds up the agricultural process. Likewise, there are spiritual methods to enlighten the process of birth and rebirth. Isn't time a concept applicable only to the physical world?

When you are conscious of the soul's essential transcendence of physical dimensions, you are beyond the confines of time. But if you don't have this awareness — if you are operating from ignorance — you are subject to time, even though you have the potential to transcend it. We know that space is not limited by the walls of a room. But space, not being conscious, is incapable of extending itself to its vast expanse outside until an external agency brings the walls down. It stays confined within concrete boundaries. It is the same with us. Physical time is incapable of liberating our soul. But knowledge has liberating power. The liberation that heightened consciousness leads to is called *jivan mukti*, liberation from biological life. If we remain ignorant of our true nature, we remain in bondage to our body nature with its trappings of *kama* — sexual desire, *krodha* — anger, *lobha* — non-restraint and *moha* — greed. True knowledge liberates whereas ignorance binds.

That Mysterious Ingredient

Anant G Nadkarni

n all walks of life, dealing with information, files, daily work or commuting is increasingly becoming central to our existence. Over time, it becomes a way of being, a sort of 'mentality' and one kind of our *samsara*. The *Bhagavad Gita* suggests that all actions, in the end, enhance knowledge. Should this apply to our routine? Jim Collins in a more 'management' milieu says 'good is the enemy of great'. Is there enough commitment to continuous improvement or pursuit of excellence? Is there that much search for more meaning, satisfaction or to actualize bigger purpose?

Knowledge-management guru Ikujiro Nonaka states that traditional information and analysis help decisions but only to some extent; and shows how tacit engagement between members of a family, colleagues or fraternity at training outfits builds higher levels of trust where deeper insights can be shared and so richer substance creates better decisions. Therefore, experience and knowledge-creating companies generated more breakthroughs. This is also true for critical business decisions and acquisitions when one set of 'managers' is typically comfortable with traditional 'analysis' while others forge far ahead by some other way! Are we really familiar with the use of more knowledge creating attributes like intuition, creativity and courage of conviction, entrepreneurship, networking or perhaps spirituality to bear more upon our lives? Is trust increasing or decreasing in our relationships and at workplaces?

Consider the word 'Upanishad'. It means the guru and disciple are in close communion. The scriptures elaborate: *Adyapana* is when the guru instructs; *adhyena* is when the disciple listens and learns with humility; *abhyasa* is to practise and reflect; *anushthana* is to internalize, become resolute, and then *anubhava* is to experience. But, before *anubhava,* there is also *anugraha* which seems slightly out of place with the other steps.

Anugraha means blessing, benediction and grace. The guru can only empower and the *shishya* is in a state of surrender. Now why and whose *anugraha* should be there? Marie Curie finds solutions in sleep. Archimedes 'gets it' in a state of relaxation! So, the tipping point of that 'eureka' moment is really not in the 'realm of power' — either of a guru or leader or just in the competence and efforts of a disciple. It is more about how the whole universe works in a kind of synchronicity conspiring to bring disparate forces into one kind of totality in an innovation or in nirvana. It cannot be expressed in words or transferred like a tangible. Gautama Buddha's three questions on old-age, disease and death did trigger a good-to-great process but disappeared in nirvana. There were no typical one, two and three pat answers to those questions. Instead, for a long time he was just speechless; then he smiled and simply raised a lotus flower. In all psychospiritual processes there is: 1) An intensity to let go of the mundane, seekers typically cross some 'river, sea or journey' of *samsara;* 2) a 'good is the enemy of great' calling for deep-seated transformation happens. 3) Universal benediction co-creating oneness makes duality and diversity disappear. Its source may be difficult to unearth or remains unknown so we tend to 'personify' the guru and more, though J Krishnamurti said the guru is just a 'signpost'. Something mysterious restores the true nature of divinity as if putting many pieces together held by mortals like us.

Like the River & Ocean

Sri Chinmoy

n the highest state of *samadhi,* when you look at other people, what kind of consciousness do you feel in them? When one is in the highest transcendental *samadhi,* the physical personality of others disappears. We do not see others as human beings. We see only a flow of consciousness, like a river that is entering into the ocean. He who is in the highest trance becomes the ocean, and he who is in a lower state of consciousness is the river. The river flows into the sea and becomes one with the sea. The one who is enjoying the highest *samadhi* does not notice any individuality or personality in others. A human being who is not in this state of *samadhi* is a flowing river of consciousness, while the one who is in *samadhi* has become the sea itself, the sea of peace and light.

Do you teach your disciples any specific technique for attaining *samadhi?*

No. *Samadhi* is a very high state of consciousness. If the beginner comes to kindergarten and asks the teacher how he can study for his Master's degree, the teacher will simply laugh. He will say, "How can I tell you?" Before we are ready to try to attain *samadhi,* we have to go through many inner spiritual experiences. Then there comes a time when the Master sees that the student is ready to enter into *savikalpa samadhi* or a temporary state of dissolution. *Nirvikalpa samadhi* or absolute dissolution is out of the question for seekers right now. One has to be a most advanced seeker before he can even think of attaining *savikalpa samadhi.*

Nirvikalpa samadhi one gets only in the highest stage of aspiration. Some disciples are very sincere and devoted, and make very fast progress; but the time has yet to come for them to think of entering into *samadhi.* For all seekers I wish to say that the spiritual ladder has quite a few rungs. We have to climb up one step at a time. *Samadhi,* for my disciples and for the vast majority of spiritual seekers on earth, is a far cry right now.

Why does a seeker need a guru?

Without a guru, your progress will be slow and uncertain. You may get high, elevating experiences and not give them adequate significance. Or doubt may enter your mind, and you may think, "I am just an ordinary person, so how can I have that kind of experience? Perhaps I am deluding myself." Or you will tell your friends about your experiences, and they will say, "It is all a mental hallucination!" But if there is someone who knows what the inner reality is, he will be able to assure you that the experiences which you have are absolutely real.

The Master encourages the seeker and inspires him. And if the seeker is doing something wrong in his meditation, the Master is in a position to correct him. Once you complete a course, you no longer need a teacher. If you want to learn how to sing, you go to a singer and learn from him. If you want to be a dancer, you go to a dancer. Once you become a good singer or dancer, you don't have to go to the teacher anymore. In the spiritual life it is the same. You need help in the beginning, but once you become extremely advanced, you will not need anybody's help.

Let Go & Rejoice

Sri M

To live amicably in society we need to be able to communicate well. One of the deterrents to good communication is anger. A feeling of emptiness always follows anger. Anger takes all that you have within you and so you are left vacuous and dissipated in its wake. Different methods are there to help us tackle our anger, but that is only anger management. It does not get to the root.

To combat anger we have to understand the reasons for it before treating it. A verse in the *Gita* says that our sense organs are always seeking sensory pleasures and objects that give pleasure. The seeking develops into an attachment, even an obsession. Naturally, then you like to possess that which you desire and in the desire to possess, anger has its roots. The desire to possess may be related to a person, object or situation. Till the desire is fulfilled, anger comes to support in the struggle to possess. It may come as a means of self-defence but becomes so powerful that it makes you forget your moorings and gradually even your memory. You lose touch with yourself. You forget who you are. That is why when a person is angry he behaves in a fashion that is uncharacteristic of him. A good example is road rage.

An angry man has poor memory. With loss of memory, by losing touch with yourself, by forgetting who you really are, you lose your mental balance. You no longer think straight. The root cause for all this is desire. True, it is difficult to live a life completely free of anger. But once we are aware of the cause of anger and the route it takes to ruin our life, we become wary of getting angry. Krishna, who was giving the above advice, did know that it is difficult to follow. Yet, because it is difficult to follow, we cannot forget about it. We have to remember it at all times as the reason why simple life and living have been held in such high esteem. That is why our life and philosophy have been formulated such that we keep desire to its minimum.

If you are deeply satisfied then there are no expectations, no desires. That is why the Ishavasya Upanishad says *'Tena tyaktena bhunjita'* — Let go and rejoice. When you let go, your dimensions are becoming bigger. It is difficult to let go, but small attempts can definitely be made. What should one let go? One should let go of all hurtful and painful memories. Stop carrying anything of yesterday into today. Otherwise regret and pain follow us like shadows. Life itself has a tendency to let go, then why are we clinging to thoughts and ideas of the past? If we let go, there is peace instantaneously, then why carry that burden?

I find that when I meet people for the first time, there is difficulty in communication. That is because we are each clinging to an image of ourselves. We are not communicating from within. Once we let go of that image, we are open and are able to communicate immediately. Even if one person lets go, the other will also automatically do so sooner than later. This will also prevent the veil of anger from ever obstructing the mind.

Teach Head, Hand & Heart

Dada J P Vaswani

he great teacher of Palestine said, "Judge a tree by its fruits,". Judged by its fruits, our current education system has failed miserably. A new type of education is needed, an education which should be related to life, real life. Education must not be merely academic or abstract: it must not aim at stuffing the student with information acquired from dead books or a set of sterile moralities and superficial values. True education should equip the student to cope adequately with life, with what lies ahead of him so that he may become a worthy participant in the adventure of life.

Intellect has developed but reverence is lacking. Critical faculties are given free play and sympathy, the power that binds and builds, is receding. Knowledge without sympathy does more harm than good. It makes us suspicious and cynical. Ideals that inspired education in ancient India must be rediscovered and introduced in our educational institutions, if we are to make our contributions to civilization and to the freshness of human life.

The number of schools and colleges and universities in India is multiplying. Graduates and holders of doctorates are increasing. Knowledge has spread. But have we grown in freshness, vitality and strength? Have we become more appreciative of the deeper values which alone give meaning and significance to life? Or do we feel bored, cut off from great ideals, hearts bereft of the song of sacrifice? A new type of education is needed — an education which will not merely develop brain power, but an education which will give a triple training of the head, hand and heart.

Nation-building is character-building. What is wanted is not mere intellectual improvement but education that helps us become whole. The final end of education is not the gain of scholarship or erudition, power or financial independence. For all these without self-discipline and self-control could well transform to becoming anti-social forces. The object of education would be to form character.

135

Ancient Indic *guru-shishya parampara* was a beautiful blend of discipline and emotion. Today, students receive information but not much by way of training of emotions. Communion with nature was another part of *ashram* life. It developed the aesthetic side of the student's life; it purified the heart.

True education is not dead knowledge; it is pulsating with life. *Vidya* or education is the search for the spiritual centre of life. *Vidya* is culture and this is possible with mental and physical discipline. Today, knowledge has made us cynical. Education is analytical and critical, but lacks power for the creative life of society. It has made alliance with secularism, with utilitarianism, with 'getting on'. The problem of education will not be solved unless knowledge is related to a Spiritual Synthesis of Life, to what is called Adhyatma Vidya. There has been too much organization of the machinery of education. We have given too much time to the study of processes and too little time to their ends and values. Organization has brought with it officialism, and officialism is the death of true culture.

A sound theory of education is a theory of ideals — the values and means by which they may be secured. The ideal is a vital idea. It is dynamic. The ideal shows the principle of infinite vitality. Thus ideals shape our lives.

Waiting & Watching

Swami Brahmdev

ne of the most beautiful aspects of human nature is our ability to wait for something. We are always waiting for something or the other. Waiting, however, is not to be seen as a distasteful activity; you must know how to wait. There are different ways of waiting and different reasons for waiting.

When we do not know how to live in the present and are always waiting, it is a reflection of our lazy nature. The lazier you are, the more unconscious of yourself you are, the more you live on the surface, in the outward appearance and with your surface nature, and you tend to simply wait. This is inertia. In this inertia we always wait for something to change hoping that somebody will come and give us what we desire.

Human nature is like that. If you observe yourself, you will see that life is always knocking on your door, every day, every minute. It is telling you to change. But you have no courage to change; you are waiting for change to happen. You just won't be the change you want. We all want peace, harmony and happiness. But how many actually work towards achieving these?

Nature is often at the receiving end — human activity gives rise to exploitation of resources and pollution, for instance. Nature wants you to change, but you don't. You are waiting (for what?) and when things get out of hand, disasters might take place. Call them natural or human-made; the fact is that the environment has its threshold and one day we are faced with a challenging situation. Sometimes it takes us by complete surprise; it comes as a shock. Catastrophesm happen and we are not entirely prepared to face the consequences.

However, sometimes we learn from these catastrophes and even take steps to bring about change — in ourselves and the environment. The day you understand that you have to cooperate, collaborate, exercise patience and feel connected, that day becomes the beginning of a new way of life.

137

If you do not have patience and do not cooperate but cry and complain, nothing much will happen except that you will allow nature to use a bigger and more powerful hammer to knock you awake.

Waiting is good but if you know how to wait. The Mother of Aurobindo Ashram said that when you know how to wait you put time by your side; time comes with you. Learn how to wait with patience and in silence. Generally, when we wait we do so full of nervous energy and tension, we are out of balance. When we are waiting we have no patience in that waiting. The difference between waiting for change and waiting with patience is that in the latter you have done what is expected of you. You have done your duty. Then one can wait with patience and put time by one's side. That can give you better and faster possibilities in life. That way time becomes your partner and helps you reach the desired result. If you have a wish, you should also have patience. Every seed wants to grow, but it is only with patience that it becomes a big tree.

Normally, however, we are waiting for change which means waiting for someone to bring in that change; for somebody else to come and clean up the mess; for someone else to take the initiative to take positive steps. This is an endless wait.

Kshama: Please Forgive Me

Anupama Jain

A friend's special forgiveness card is lying in front of me. It says:
"I can't change past misdeeds,
But can learn from them,
Making amends and starting anew
For whatever mistakes I might have made
Knowingly or unknowingly with thoughts, words or deeds
That caused you hurt and pain,
Please forgive me and let us start on, afresh."

She was a dear friend, but due to a misunderstanding we parted ways; now this card brought tears to my eyes, washing away all bitterness and that too, on the concluding day of Paryushan Parva or Das Lakshan Dharm Parva. It's the most auspicious Jain festival, observed for 10 days in Chaturmas, a celebration of human values including forgiveness, nonviolence and truthfulness.

Kshama is termed as 'veerasya abhushanam' — a strength, and not weakness. We cannot reverse the past; to look ahead we need to forgive and move on. On the auspicious day of Kshamavani Parva, members of the Jain community request their relatives and friends to pardon them for any mistakes committed knowingly or unknowingly; if they have hurt them by way of speech, deed or thought.

Tirthankar Mahavira said, "Forgiveness is spiritual purification, it is uplift of Soul." Forgiveness reveals high morale. It is a jewel worn by noble souls. Mahavira said, "The one whom you hurt or kill is you. All souls are equal and alike and have the similar nature and qualities. Anger begets more anger and forgiveness and love lead to more forgiveness and love."

Forgiveness is a boon for the one who forgives and the one who is forgiven. Forgiveness has been regarded the basis of all types of penance and meditation, but in the material world also, from the scientific and psychological viewpoint, forgiveness is believed to bestow physical vitality. It can help cure disease and engender mental development. Jainism says that forgiveness is gifted by the one who forgives, earned by the one seeking it, and is natural as part of our celestial nature.

Forgiveness can be earned by request or prayer, *pratikramana* or confession and repentance, and *prayashchitta* or willingness to suffer consequences. It could be described as a healing mantra to help us lead a healthy lifestyle free of anger, gloom, worry and hatred.

Forgiveness is part of *ahimsa* or non-violence; it helps us triumph over anger and hatred and makes us more content and healthy. MK Gandhi forgave his assassin even as he was dying. Jesus Christ, when crucified, prayed to God to pardon his tormentors as they 'know not what they do'. In Buddhism, forgiveness is seen as a practice to avert harmful emotions from causing havoc on one's mental well-being. In Islam, Allah is described as 'the most forgiving'. Hindu thought describes forgiveness as the highest virtue. Jains celebrate this great virtue as a celebratory ritual, as it is such an integral part of life.

All religions advocate forgiveness for it gives s strength; hence forgiveness is not to be seen as a sign of weakness or guilt. It is a divine attribute — hence the saying, 'To err is human, to forgive divine'.

Here's a prayer: God, forgive us for all our transgressions and mistakes and may all *jivas,* all beings including the environment remain peaceful, harmonious and coexist without conflict.

Contemplation & Compassion

Pranav Khullar

he ancients believed that at the heart of a truly intelligent mind and at the core of a democratic discourse lies the cardinal virtue of compassion that can help us rise above our deepest dislikes and prejudices. Beyond the matrix of our vanities lies this concept of karuna or compassionate wisdom, which allows us to understand and love the other.

Buddhist scriptures narrate the story of sage Asanga, founder of the Yogachara school, who had mastered the intellectual aspects of the ancient texts and the *sutras,* but who felt an enormous emptiness, still. Even his long meditations left him more lonely than alone and completely disheartened, so he decided to give up all practices.

Reportedly, on his way back to the town he saw a dog whose body was being eaten up by maggots. Overcome by compassion, he resolved to remove the maggots but found it was not possible to do so. In an act of sacrifice, Asanga decided to cut the flesh from his own thigh to attract the worms away from the dog. When that also did not work, he decided to transport the worms to his own flesh by body contact. At that moment the dog disappeared and Lord Maitreya stood in front of Asanga. Lord Maitreya told Asanga that his fervent practice needed to be grounded in universal compassion to enable him to see that the Self he sought was omnipresent.

The ennobling principle is characterised by J Krishnamurti as the essence of intelligence as distinct from intellect, from which arises the capacity to love. A truly intelligent mind is one which can comprehend and experience the sorrow of another as one's own — and in this experience, the mind 'feels' the interconnectedness of life, beyond the limited i-me-mine thought process which has conditioned us. *Karuna* is the great spiritual force which separates the evolved from the not-so-evolved, helping us to reach a more mature *jignasa* state of mind where it becomes easier to understand the deeper purpose of life and existence.

The need to cultivate compassion is central to traditions worldwide, but the Buddhist traditions formalize and conceptualize the principle as a psychological tool to cultivate liking and equanimity for all beings as a psycho-meditative technique in itself. It is the defining characteristic of a Bodhisattva, the heroic soul who puts his nirvana state of mind on indefinite hold in order to help others evolve on the path to understanding. Buddha saw the need to cultivate compassion as the trigger to develop detachment — a paradoxical but a commonsense way to induce a detached attitude, detached from the limitations of one's own mind-matrix, by trying to understand the larger whole. And then, at some point of the journey, you need to detach yourself from the fabric of the whole as well, to try and understand the design behind the complex code of life.

The interconnectedness of life can be felt only by a compassionate heart which would see beyond the misconceptions and the limitations of the thought-mind, which, as the Dalai Lama says, "...itself (the limited mind) predetermines what we perceive..." Compassion is the healing meditative tool to tear away the veil of ignorance that makes us think we are all separate entities. The contemplative path and the path of compassion are really one.

The Grand Illusion

Rajiv Vij

ne fish said to the other, "Do you believe in this ocean that they talk about?" This Chinese saying illustrates how narrow our vision of the world and the universe can be. We see the world from our limited perceptual framework. Despite an overwhelming evolution of the human race, the human mind is severely restricted by what it can perceive through the senses.

What we hear is limited by the frequencies our ears can process — dogs can hear many higher frequencies and hence have a very different perception of the same sounds. Our sight is limited by the light frequencies our eyes can relate to; since pit vipers can sense heat from infrared rays they must construct the same world rather differently. If we had a different receiver mechanism, we would be hearing other frequencies and seeing in new ways.

With scientific knowledge, we know that many things are not what they appear to be — the sky isn't blue, only the scattering of the blue light absorbed by the atmosphere makes it appear so; the moon doesn't rise in the night; and the house we live in is not stationary, but rotates along with the earth. Essentially, we see, hear and process what we can and not what reality is.

Truth realization is not easy. Besides the difficulty, our perceptions are further clouded by our personal thoughts and emotions. A Buddhist verse says: "Is anything on earth universally and unanimously recognized as beautiful? For a lover, a beautiful woman is an object of desire; for the hermit, a distraction; for the wolf, a good meal." What is the truth, then? Everything in the universe is made up of energy. All beings are manifestations of the same energy. This vital spiritual force breathes life into every living being and sustains every cell and organism. It's like an enormous field of colourless and odourless energy which encompasses everything and every being that we can imagine — all of that existing, not in isolation or in separation, but in one continuum.

What appears solid is only so because of the frequency of wavelengths that our senses are capable of perceiving. Our minds create a three-dimensional world from this continuum of free-flowing energy, comprising of electrons and neutrons. Like the fish in the Chinese saying, when we cannot see this continuum, we are limited to noticing the individual parts of the creation. As a result, the trees, animals, humans and all other objects seem disjointed from us. 'I' as an individual does not exist, never existed, never will — the sense of 'I' is merely a perception of our limited mind.

From Einstein we know that matter and energy are interchangeable; they're essentially one. When broken down to its barest form, all matter is the same energy. We can break a glass jar into pieces but each piece, however small, will still be glass. Similarly, know that God is in each one of us, and we are part of the same whole. This knowledge can set us free.

As we make a conscious effort to stay connected with this realization, we become better equipped to playing the roles of our life — businessman, teacher, wife, father and friend — with tremendous happiness and inner peace. This connection lets us be like an actor who plays her role on stage with great sincerity but stays conscious of the fact that she is really not the character she's playing — and thus not overly identify with the fortunes and misfortunes of her given role!

How to Eradicate Corruption

Maulana Wahiduddin Khan

o eradicate corruption we require individuals who are incorruptible and, undoubtedly, what produces such individuals is spirituality. There is a saying that violence begins in the mind. This is true also of corruption: corruption begins in the mind. If we can alter our thinking, we can safely say that we shall have eradicated corruption by at least 50 per cent. What changes the heart and mind for the better is spirituality. When an airplane takes off, it leaves behind everything and reaches a higher plane, at which point it is capable of flying towards its destination without any hurdles. Similarly, a spiritual seeker is able to fly to a higher plane where he is free of negative influences.

There are two aspects to spirituality: theory and practice. Basically, spirituality is a non-materialistic approach to life's issues as opposed to the other approach that is based on materialistic interest. The root cause of corruption is the materialistic approach.

Applied spirituality enables one to infuse daily life with spiritual values and those who do so are able to distance themselves from all kinds of corrupt practices. One aspect of applied spirituality is the duty-consciousness which it induces. A rights-conscious person can see only what is in his own interest, while the duty-conscious person looks to the well-being of others and, in doing so, can never stoop to corrupt practices.

How to inculcate spirituality among people? Basically, it is a part of education, both formal and informal. Education means mind training, with special emphasis on inculcating high values. To spread spiritual values in society, we need value-based education, especially during schooling, which is a preparatory period for life, and if we want to build a spiritual society, we must adopt a value-based education.

A spiritual perspective makes one evaluate actions in terms of their results — a major factor in having a sense of responsibility.

One who cultivates such a perspective is able to see things in terms of value. He is able to differentiate between right and wrong.

There is a saying: "A wise man is one who knows the relative value of things." A wise person is one who has a predictable character. All these qualities stem from spiritual training. It is the responsibility of reformers, therefore, to train people to become duty-conscious — for a duty-conscious person can never involve himself in any negative activity such as corruption. Spirituality helps keep emotions under control and brings peace of mind. An education system that includes spiritual values in instruction will help students imbibe eternal values and truths that enable them to not only develop their intellectual capacity but also to fulfil their role as responsible human beings in society.

A materialistic person is more concerned with material than with spiritual goals or values. Corruption is a phenomenon of a materialistic society while spirituality is a phenomenon of evolved persons. It is only such persons who can build a non-corrupt society. Spirituality and corruption cannot go together.

If a society is to be free of corruption, it has to be made up of evolved or, at least, evolving individuals who have a fairly strong sense of what is right and what is wrong. This is the only solution to the problem of corruption. This is the right beginning and only the right beginning can make it possible to reach the desired goal.

Fuel That's Available in Plenty

PV Vaidyanathan

f life is a journey, and the human being is the vehicle, then the best fuel for a successful completion of this journey is love. This is a secret that is known to all, but implemented by few. And when we substitute some other emotion and make it our fuel, the vehicle cannot perform as well as it should. The journey of life is then no longer smooth, but becomes jumpy, noisy, bouncy, uncomfortable and prone to frequent breakdowns, and constantly needing help from others to set it right.

Unlike fossil fuels which are used in actual vehicles, the fuel called love is available in plenty and is unlikely to become depleted. Every human being born on this planet is a source of this fuel called love. He is capable of loving 24X7. Love is our natural state. Unfortunately, this natural state gets corrupted, resulting in adulterated fuel being produced and used to run life.

Love works slowly as compared to its opposite emotions, fear and hate. Though love is natural, hate and fear come to us more easily. If you want to get a group of people together for a common cause and under a common banner, love for something might take you years to unite them. Hate and fear can work in a matter of minutes. Hence, the natural enemies of love are much more powerful and appealing. Love appeals to the true being or soul, while the mind thrives on hate and fear.

Why does fear predominate our lives, when we all know that love is the true fuel of life? This is where the mind comes in. Our true being or spirit thrives only on love. But between our spirit and body is another important entity, the mind.

The control of our lives, instead of being in the hands of the spirit, has been taken over by the mind. And the mind is a very complex entity. It is logical and illogical, rational and irrational, good and bad, loving and hating, giving and grabbing, killing and rescuing, full of hope and help, while also filled with hopelessness and helplessness, simultaneously. The mind is a paradox, unpredictable and unknown, with its own way of functioning. It is volatile and restless, but yet, it constantly seeks peace, stillness and stability.

To be with the mind means our lives would be like a roller-coaster ride. The stability and stillness that we seek in our lives, the rest and relaxation that we crave, the peace and calmness that we desperately need, are not to be found in the arena of the mind. If they are found, they will come coupled with their respective opposites. This is the duality of life. Duality is always of the mind. The spirit or soul is always one. And it needs only one fuel and that is love.

One cannot get love without first giving love. That is the law of Nature. In existence, giving comes before receiving, sowing comes before reaping. But most of us seek and hope to receive without wanting to give. So, first give love if you want to be loved. And then we will receive love, a thousand times more.

It needs us only to take the first small step of giving. The Buddha used to say to his disciples, "If you knew what I know, about the power of giving, you would not have a single meal in your life without first sharing it with someone."

You Don't Have to Be Stupid

Swami Sukhabodhananda

I don't have the intelligence to live life wisely, is there a way out?

You are humble enough to ask me this question. Your humility is not an act of stupidity. Secondly, you acknowledge you have been stupid, and any recognition of weakness is a part of strength. Thirdly, being aware of one's helplessness will open up new possibilities of grace. Life is a combination of ignorance and knowledge. It needs fine-tuning. You have knowledge but if it is not polished with humility and understanding, then such knowledge will not bless you.

Look at life with awareness. Everyone at some level is stupid, is helpless and this recognition helps us to act wisely. If people think, "I know, I need not change," such knowledge will bind a person and not free him.

First, don't conclude you don't have intelligence. God has given us this intelligence. But we have to log on to it. You have the power to see, hear, feel, walk and digest and all this is an act of intelligence. The bird has the intelligence to build a beautiful nest, which can protect it from rain. Where did this intelligence come from? It is hidden in us.

Imagine the bird saying, "I can't talk like a man," and feeling miserable... then it will not validate the power to build a nest which is like a waterproof residence. Many of man-made houses leak despite waterproofing.

The greedy mind invalidates the riches of life. So drop this conclusion, "I am not intelligent; I am stupid." 'I am stupid' should not be a conclusion but something to be worked on.

What is stupidity?

Stupidity is unawareness. You are unaware and act as though you know. Drop this drama. Foolishness is a sleep you live in. You can always wake up. Out of this sleep, you dream and then take the

149

dream to be real. This sleep, filled with dreams, superimposes the world outside and you only see the superimposition. Like how a snake is superimposed on the rope and then you only see the snake and not the rope.

Problems do not make you stupid. A problem is an alarm system which says, act on it and be creative to solve it. Every problem is an invitation for us to be creative. Don't exaggerate a problem or underestimate it or become indifferent to it. When adventurous energy in you is missing, then you feel this pain.

We have both male and female energies in us. Male energy represents adventure while female energy represents compassion. Balance the two. Go trekking, take up a sport, be in the company of people who have adventurous energy.

Is not the basic problem the fear of death?

Death is happening at every moment. Yesterday is dead and you are born today in the present. Death has never been an enemy. The real enemy is your non-acceptance of the flow of life and your rigidity on how life should be. You have treated death as an end of life; in fact, it is a door to a new beginning. Be happy with the door and do not bang yourself against the door. People have an answer in spite of being wrong. An answer does not change our life; living and acting wisely does.

Experience the Truth

Sreeram Manoj Kumar

Knowledge of scriptures might bring a sense of accomplishment and happiness but unless our attitude is flawless and our conscience clear, it will be hard to achieve steadfastness and bliss. However much one is well versed in the Vedas, Upanishads and the *Bhagavad Gita* — and even if a person has *shlokas* at her fingertips, she must possess control over her senses, limit her desires and contemplate the knowledge she has, to attain spiritual progress. Ravana had unmatched knowledge but his attitude was not good.

The continuous chain of trials and tribulations of various degrees of magnitude in life could help a seeker understand the meaning and purpose of life. An ignorant person blames either God or destiny or even more so her family and friends for all that happens to her.

A man wants his young son to learn swimming. He takes him to the nearby lake to give him lessons on how to swim. He first ties an inflatable tube to his waist, so that it lets him float. After some days the boy is familiar with the upthrust got by the arm cycle and leg kick, and he experiences buoyancy. When the father is confident that the boy can float without the help of the tube, he removes it and lets the boy swim without the help of the tube. An inflatable swimming tube only helps the boy to remain afloat on the surface of the water; it only assists him in learning how to swim. Likewise, scriptures help us to get a vision; we get a vivid account of the glory and splendour of the omnipresence, omniscience and omnipotence of the Absolute Truth. However, ultimately we can progress on the spiritual path only by our own effort.

There are many scholars and pundits who boast and want to prove that the philosophy that they follow is superior to that of others. These philosophies are like the materials used to keep the boy floating in water. While one person uses an inflatable tube to keep afloat, others have used the dried, unpunctured bottle gourd, some use thermocol blocks, some others use float boards. What is important is that the student needs to learn how to swim, how to keep afloat — it does not matter what the aids used are. No one will ever ask us what type of material we had used to keep ourselves afloat while we were learning to swim. It is the same with philosophies also; the main criterion is to reach the goal.

Truth is one but the means to know it are numerous. Hence, the facts regarding the Truth are many. Facts are not self-explanatory; they are analysed by theories and theses may differ from each other. We have accumulated vast mounds of information about the Truth, but very few have experienced the Truth.

Truth which is absolute can never be comprehended by the human mind since it is relative. It is impossible to know the Absolute Truth although by the uninterrupted *sadhana* and grace of the guru, the Self can experience it. Truth thus experienced is but our own experience. This is a universal law which, if understood, can take us to Bliss, eternal happiness. We are that Self which is comprehensive, composite, part of Cosmic Consciousness and therefore immortal and infinite — beyond death and destruction. Awareness of this is the experience of Truth.

Sink or Swim in the Sea of Life

Mangesh Ghogre

fter years of gazing wistfully at the pool, I recently decided to brave it and take the plunge. Learning to swim was an interesting experience and, to top it all, I found it gave me new spiritual insight! First, learning in general helps you stay afloat in life. Fear of drowning is one reason why many hesitate to learn swimming. Similarly, for fear of failure, we hesitate to dream big or pursue ambitions. We worry about getting drowned in a sea of challenges, problems and roadblocks. We think the world is out there to take us down.

To return to the pool, I now realize that water is not a threat; in fact water helps us survive. Breathing is second nature to us; hence it is a big challenge for water to drown us. I am surprised at how well our body is equipped with natural survival instincts to help us float and not drown. All we have to do is to use that potential to stay afloat.

In life, each one of us is blessed with unique survival skills that we call talent. We need to appreciate these virtues which shall help us swim in the sea of life. Instead of fearing getting drowned, one should drown fear itself. Swimming then will come to be as easy as breathing.

My second lesson came when I learned how to coordinate my hand and leg movements. My hands had to push the water back so I could swim ahead. This was akin to overcoming hindrances in life's path, in order to make progress. The more water we push behind, the farther we swim. Even more important is the principle that when my hand movements get streamlined with movement in water, progress is faster and smoother.

Therefore, when we handle problems in alignment with our strengths and weaknesses, we handle those problems better. On the other hand, when we are just splashing water and are not making best use of our talents or find ourselves in the 'wrong job', we encounter frustration or failure. All the more reason for us to understand our strengths and accordingly align our goals and ambitions.

Lessons from the leg movement also did not go unnoticed. Contrary to the backward hand push, the legs have to be moved downwards. Basically, the more you push the water down, the more you remain up. This goes contrary to popular understanding that to float one has to push or hold the body up.

An instance of seeing this fallacy in action is when a person who does not know how to swim is scrambling to stay afloat. I learnt that if one just keeps pushing the water down, it is hard for the person to drown. Just as if we continue to keep pushing negative thoughts down, we will continue to keep our chin up and so stay afloat. When we panic, we lose sight of this simple principle.

The symphony of swimming occurs when hand and leg movements are in tandem. If the movements are not in sync, either we tend to drown or we don't move ahead much. Similarly, when we align our strengths to push obstacles behind, stay enthusiastic and push down negative thoughts, swimming in the sea of life seems so effortless. This in a way is akin to our own ego becoming one with that of the water.

Worship as Act of Living

Swami Atmashraddhananda

orship or adoration of the Divine has the potential to bring one nearer to God. This could take many forms — rituals, prayer, chanting, service and contemplation, to name a few. What is important, however, is how intensely you seek God.

Ramakrishna, the saint of Dakshineshwar, Kolkata, was a priest at the Kali temple. But he was no ordinary priest. Curious as a child, he would ask, looking at the deity, "Does the Divine Mother really exist? Or is this image merely a stone?" He also wept and cried to his 'Mother', the Mother of the Universe, to reveal Herself to him. He entreated Her to uncover the veil of ignorance that kept Her away from him. "O Mother, do you really exist? Show me, then!"

His prayers were intense and deeply devotional. One day, fed up of waiting, he gave the deity an ultimatum: "If You don't reveal Yourself to me, I will end my life!" And the Mother did appear before him.

Recounting the divine experience, Ramakrishna said, "I used to worship the deity in the Kali temple. It was suddenly revealed to me that everything is pure spirit — the utensils, altar, door frame — all pure spirit. All beings are pure spirit. Then, like a madman, I began to shower everything I saw with flowers; whatever I saw, I worshipped!"

In this manner, Ramakrishna's worship culminated in his vision of the all-pervasive Divinity that is the foundation of Creation. He no longer restricted his worship to an image; it became an act of living. He said, "One day, while worshipping Shiva, I was about to place a Bel leaf on the head of the image when it was revealed to me that this Virat, the Universe, is itself Shiva. After that I stopped my worship of Shiva's image. Another day I was plucking flowers when it was revealed to me in a flash that flowering plants were so many bouquets...each plant was a bouquet adorning the universal form of God. That was the end of my plucking flowers. I look on the human being just the same way. When I see an individual, I see God Himself walking on earth..."

Ramakrishna's vision of the all-pervasive reality of God is a testimony of what spiritual masters have realized and taught since long. True worship is to realize that every individual is essentially divine. We see others only as good or bad, ugly or beautiful, rich or poor and we treat them accordingly. We miss out the essential core of being, which is divinity. True worship is when we see God in everyone. If worship of God is restricted only to an image, neglecting God's living images (all beings), such worship is incomplete and imperfect.

Ramakrishna's disciple Vivekananda observed, as if elaborating on his guru's spiritual experience: "If you cannot see God in the human face, how can you see Him in the clouds, or in images made of dull, dead matter, or in mere fictitious stories of our brain? When you see man as God, everything, even the tiger, will be welcome. Whatever comes to you is but the Lord, the Eternal, the Blessed One, appearing to us in various forms, as our father, mother, friend and child — they are our own soul playing with us."

Honesty & Diplomacy

PV Vaidyanathan

We have always been taught that honesty is the best policy, and that to lie is a bad thing to do. As we grow older, we realize that in many situations it is a good idea to keep quiet or, better still, be diplomatic and tactfully handle sensitive issues. The line dividing honesty and diplomacy is a thin one. We have to be careful in deciding when to be honest and when to be at our diplomatic best. We also have to decide whether we should be absolutely candid, or use the truth as a matter of convenience.

Our relationships demand complete honesty, or else, we get into trouble. In a household, for instance, the oldest member Suresh was quite diplomatic in commenting on the new cook's unpalatable creations. Whatever he would cook, the cook would always be told that the food was 'not bad'. Suresh would avoid criticizing the cook for the mediocre food he dished out. The situation worsened to a point when what was cooked was almost inedible. Suresh could not take it anymore and screamed at the cook for serving such bad-tasting food. The cook was taken aback. From that day onwards, everything that Suresh had diplomatically papered over started to show huge cracks. Daily fights and arguments became the order of the day and, one fine day, the cook simply left.

Therefore, diplomacy or lack of honesty can lead to deterioration in our relationships. Before you decide to be totally frank, you must carefully analyse all consequences of your actions. While life needs a good mix of honesty and diplomacy, when to be honest and when to be diplomatic is a tough individual choice. Whatever we do must make us comfortable, peaceful and happy. An honest person will feel frustrated and restless when forced to be diplomatic against his will, while a diplomatic one will get highly stressed at the thought of speaking the plain truth. How to react in a situation also depends on what is at stake. If you want to be honest and speak your mind against your boss, you better be prepared to lose your job. If you tell your friend what you hate about him, it might end your friendship. Once you are ready to accept the consequences without regret or remorse, then you can be honest.

Why do we become diplomatic when we know the obvious truth? Diplomacy is always an escape hatch that we use to avoid hurting others and ourselves. When the boy asks his girlfriend: "Am I looking fat?" and the girl answers honestly, "Yes, you have put on too much weight," one can well imagine her boyfriend's reactions. But if the girl speaks her mind and faces her boyfriend's wrath out of genuine affection for him, it is likely that he will take the issue of weight control seriously. Diplomacy protects us in the short-term, but it is honesty that brings long-term benefits and permanent gains.

To be completely honest, you must ask yourself, "Why am I afraid of speaking the truth?" Diplomacy is for our self-protection and self-preservation. Our egos are too fragile to accept insult and criticism. Few of us would want to rock the boat by speaking the truth at work or home. We like to avoid confrontations. Honesty and diplomacy, however, are not mutually exclusive. It takes tact and courage to speak the truth at the right time in the right manner, without being abrasive.

Wheel of Joys & Sorrows

OP Yadava

he Taoists speak of 10,000 sorrows and 10,000 joys, with the joys turning to sorrows and sorrows turning to joys without breaking a sweat. In fact, Buddhists talk of four sets of contrasting conditions that most of us will go through at various times in our lifetime, namely, praise and blame, gain and loss, pleasure and pain, and fame and disrepute, a set called 'Dhammas'. The response called for in these events, even according to our scriptures, is a balanced one, because we must be able to see their insubstantiality, impermanence and tangible nature.

Leo Tolstoy said in *War and Peace* that "pure and complete sorrow is as impossible as pure and complete joy". The more we get attached with our successes and the more we gloat in their palliative warmth, the worse will be the retribution when we fail. William Wordsworth in 'Resolution and Independence' said, "As high as we have mounted in delight, in our dejection do we sink as low."

When the Indian cricket team won the World Cup in 2011, there was an overwhelming outpouring of national joy and enthusiasm. During all the hype and celebration, few would have remembered the retribution and stone-throwing that cricketers faced after their losing a game in 2007. It, therefore, behoves the players, authorities and the public to take victory in its stride and though they may enjoy and savour the moment, they should not build sandcastles so high today that they find themselves in the adjoining trenches of their own doing tomorrow. Moments of joy will breed an equal and opposite reaction of sorrow in times to come and more often than not sorrow creeps up on one like a bad habit, sooner than one would expect.

As a society, are we mature enough to handle happiness? The way we react to disaster, tragedies and miseries in life is much more measured than our response to happiness, as was demonstrated by our much calmer, cool, calculated and measured response to tsunamis, earthquakes and other disasters; but it appears that such is not the case with happiness. Osho said, "But when happiness comes, it is as if the heavens are open for you and it is raining cats and dogs, and your small hut is just in a flood...all boundaries are lost. It is maddening."

The extreme reaction to art and culture is also a reflection of the same mindset, and the intolerance that abounds also comes from a similar attitude. It, therefore, is important that we do not go overboard but treat victory in the right spirit.

To remain unmoved by achievement and failure is a sign of balance and stability. The most significant aspect of progressing on the spiritual path is maintaining equanimity, a term which is central to every religious theme in the world. In Buddhism, we call it Upeksha; in Patanjali's Yogasutra it is mentioned as one of the four sublime attitudes; in Judaism as Menuhat Ha-Nefesh or Yashuv HaHa Ha-Da'at. In Christianity, Islam and in Hinduism, there is talk of equanimity of response as being necessary for upward evolution and graduation to a higher form. "Equanimity is not a dry neutrality or cool aloofness, but mature equanimity produces a radiance and warmth of being." So let us learn to be equanimous in both our achievements and failures, through practice of mindful response.

No Escaping the Big Boss

Seema Burman

When the rich and famous are caught cheating, the common man feels good. He feels, at last justice has prevailed. Riches bring a feeling of resentment in others unless they are available to all. The rich might flaunt their wealth. However, if we are true to our pure nature, our instinct would be to share it with others. This is selfless action. Selfish actions are condemned by all whether they are well versed in scriptures or not. It comes from loving all, arising from the feeling of devotion and the realization that the world is an illusion and nothing is mine.

A guru asked two disciples to kill two pigeons where none could witness their act. One disciple went to the forest and wrung the bird's neck and came cheerfully to the guru but the second disciple explored the whole forest, the village, nearby hills and river and came back tired saying that wherever he went he saw two eyes of the pigeon staring at him. "Those frightened eyes followed me everywhere, looking at my actions. You had said that no one should witness the killing but even when I closed its eyes, they appeared in the sun, clouds, sky, moon, water, hills, trees, birds. There was not a space where those eyes did not follow me. I could not kill it."

There is no escape from Nature. All its elements witness our actions and thoughts. That is why sages called them *devatas*. All Vedic *samskaras* are held in the presence of Nature's elements whether it is marriage, funeral or worship. Natural forces regulate the outside and the inside; *devatas* rule all our organs. No thought or action goes unnoticed. However, we can appeal for mercy, just as a convicted prisoner appeals to the president. For, isn't life, too, one big jail where we are prisoners of our own thought, action and deed?

Chanting God's name, accepting teachings of scriptures, becoming selfless, loving God and His creation, accepting all that comes our way calmly and realizing that the world is an illusion, are ways of appealing. Seeing our changed behaviour, the compassionate One reduces our suffering and we soon find that our outlook has changed and our difficulties seem so tiny.

A saint regularly visited the local jail to help inmates understand the goal of life, mystery of God and His ways. One day the jailor took him to a miserable inmate who kept saying how unjust God was. Someone had looted and murdered a village merchant with whom he was not on good terms. But since people had seen this man (the one convicted of the crime) with the victim, he was assumed to be the murderer. Due to circumstantial evidence, he was given life imprisonment.

The saint met the jailor, lawyer, neighbours and relatives of the convict and saw that everything pointed towards him. Puzzled, the saint started spending more time with the inmate. One day the inmate began recalling his earlier life in which he had caused the death of a man but escaped punishment as it was deemed to be a case of suicide. Wondered the saint: Was this man paying in this life for his past actions? Is there no escape from God's watchful eyes?

It is a difficult question to answer. However, it is beneficial to perform only such actions as are deemed to be positive — and that do not hurt another — whether one is being watched by God or not.

Social & Spiritual Impact

Anant G Nadkarni

e're all striving to improve the quality of our lives. However, very few of the attempts to bring about institutional reforms have helped leverage people power to co-create 'overall impact'. When things come to a boil, we do rise up and question the establishment and sometimes things do change for the better. But how to ensure that cumulative positive influences — whether brought about by people power or good governance — get sustained? The freedom movement that liberated India from foreign domination continues to inspire us. Hence we look up to those who provided creative and motivating leadership like MK Gandhi. There are many reasons, however, why such leaders are not commonplace.

Firstly, Gandhi's leadership was at all times at its zenith, deeply rooted in personal experimentation and interpretation of principles like ahimsa and swaraj. The concept of 'being the change' or to begin with oneself helped awaken so many people, instilling a sense of personal ownership for action that often involved immense sacrifice.

Secondly, Gandhi believed in *poorna* swaraj, complete independence, as did Lokmanya Tilak — to deal with an issue in totality. While regulation and institutional solutions are important, much more emphasis is placed on public behaviour and restraint. Gandhi constantly inspired people to believe in what they were doing and to patiently demonstrate it in some form. For him, social change evolved out of a shared vision. Development work is not seen as something that ought to deliver 'outcomes' as if an issue is just about fulfilling some sort of a 'resource gap' — say a missing piece of legislation, institutional mechanism, monetary or technological provisions. Regulatory and other ways of administration are only the means, for lasting change for the better begins with you and me.

Thirdly, Gandhi saw in us enormous humane and social potential and the huge possibility of its committed and purposeful engagement. This would also steer one away from divisive

163

tendencies like caste, creed, class and language. Gandhi then set out a strategy to involve people constructively, as a noted author and journalist observed: 1. For pious people there were *satsangs* with multi-faith prayers; 2. To ensure livelihoods there was spinning work and the whole enterprise-solution of swadeshi and khadigram; 3. For activists it was satyagraha, the principle centred on peaceful non-cooperation; 4. For journalists and others there were a variety of engagements where their views were aired with a sense of immense personal and collective responsibility. All of these summed up the message to those in power: 'Quit India'.

Ask: Do we see the need for a leadership that can mobilize people into action, beyond demanding systemic provisions? Are we aware of the need for deep, useful engagement, for people to support mechanisms of justice to bring the corrupt to book? How can we help alleviate terrorism instead of getting involved only in scientific explanation of the composition and intensity of a just-exploded bomb that destroyed lives? How many businesses will engage the poorest of the poor through their supply chains to help them take the first step of the economic ladder? Would our actions save or destroy flora and fauna? Can we ensure the safety and nurturing of women and children?

Why can't a bit of what moved Gandhi, and through him, others, rub off on us so we can take that small step forward? Perhaps then we could be the change we wish to see in the world.

The Tree's Eloquent Silence

Maulana Wahiduddin Khan

n front of my house in New Delhi there is a full-grown tree, in whose shade I am in the habit of sitting. I call it my spiritual tree. In fact, this tree is my teacher, although a silent one. The previous summer, this tree, like many other trees, shed its green leaves. Gradually, it became simply like dry wood.

I was doubtful whether it would ever again turn green. But in the spring, the whole scenario changed. My spiritual tree again became a tree with lush green foliage. The rebirth of this tree was a great lesson. My spiritual tree turned into a speaking tree. It gave me a significant message: 'Don't be hopeless in any situation. After every dry season, there is a good harvest. After every spell of hopelessness, there is new hope, and after every failure, there is a great success. After every dark night, there is a bright morning.'

My spiritual tree never left its allotted space. Neither did it ever protest against anyone; it never demanded that others find its new, living leaves. It remained at the same place and started a new process within itself. What was this process? The process was to get its food from below as well as from sunlight. The strategy worked. The whole of nature came to its aid and after some months, it gained its lost greenery once again. This is the lesson I learned from my spiritual tree. No protest, no complaint, no demand, no street activism or stage activism: simply trust your own natural abilities and work silently. Try to reshape your destiny. And very soon you will be glad to discover that you have regained your life.

What is a tree? A tree is an illustration from nature. Nature tells us of its scheme through trees — that after every winter, a new spring will follow. What is needed is only to discover that you have the power to discover your potential. Discover the opportunities around you and then avail of all these opportunities by silent planning and action.

My spiritual tree creates no noise, no problems; it creates no unwanted situations. These are the secrets of a green tree. This is also the secret of human life. Adopt the tree culture and you will be a good member of society, just like a tree which is a good 'member' of the environment.

Moreover, my spiritual tree has never asked me for anything...It has never sent any bills to my office. Yet it gives me pleasant scenery, shade, green branches, fresh oxygen, flowers, etc. It also provides a perch for chirping birds who with their beautiful songs give me a lot of pleasure.

The culture of my spiritual tree is that it silently gives me a message: 'Adopt my culture and you will become a fitting ornament of the garden of the universe.'

My spiritual tree gives me the best definition of spirituality. Live as a complex-free soul and you will find a complex-free world to live in. Your destiny is in your hands. Never allow others to decide your destiny. Utilize your opportunities, turn your potential into actuality and soon you will find that you have no complaints to register against others. Every tree is an embodiment of spirituality; a silent lexicon. So adopt the tree as your teacher. The tree is a good teacher who is available at all times to every student. The only condition for learning from the tree is the ability to listen to silence.

The Scintillating Blue Pearl

Anup Taneja

Swami Muktananda, the sage of Ganeshpuri, says that seekers should make the best of life because it is only through the human form that one can meditate intensely and rise to the highest level of consciousness, the supracausal state. Seekers who are steadfast in their practice of meditation and who have deep faith in inner self-will would eventually be able to delve deep into the subtle realms of consciousness. Here, they begin to perceive the scintillating Blue Pearl, the ultimate goal of spiritual *sadhana*.

In the initial stages of meditation, the seeker perceives the red aura that represents the gross physical body through which the waking state of consciousness is experienced with the aid of five senses of perception. The body is the vehicle by which one experiences pleasure and pain; in fact, it is through the body that sins are committed or good deeds are performed. The individual soul in the physical body is seated in the eyes and is known as *vishva,* which is represented by 'A' — the first letter of AUM, the primordial sound.

As the seeker makes further progress in meditation, he begins to perceive the white flame that represents the subtle or astral body of the size of the thumb. The dream state of consciousness is experienced through the astral body that is represented by 'U' — the second letter of AUM. The individual soul in the body is called *taijasa* and is seated in the throat.

The next stage in meditation is marked by the appearance of black light that represents the causal body through which the deep sleep state is experienced. This is a testing time for the seeker because a deep, terrifying and unending darkness is experienced in this state, forcing seekers to abandon their meditation.

The individual soul is called *prajna* which is seated in the heart and is the size of a fingertip. It is represented by the symbol 'M'— the third letter of AUM. The seeker who remains absolutely fearless in meditation and has surrendered himself unconditionally to Mother Kundalini receives Her choicest blessings. Having purified the seeker at the physical, subtle and causal levels, Shakti begins to operate at the supra-causal level within the *sahasrara* in the crown of the head where the seeker, to his utter amazement, perceives the infinitely beautiful and sparkling Blue Pearl, the size of a sesame seed. Despite being tiny, the Blue Pearl is the seed that contains the entire universe. It represents the supra-causal body through which the supra-causal state of consciousness is experienced. It moves like lightning and the seeker can see it emerging from the eyes with rapid speed. Blue Pearl is the vehicle through which the soul leaves the body after death and travels to different astral zones, depending upon one's stage of spiritual evolution.

Swami Muktananda says: "One day, after the Blue Pearl has remained steady for a long time, it will expand infinitely, and its light will fill the universe. Then, with intense wonder, you will see that the whole universe is shimmering and scintillating with the Blue Light. You will realize that you yourself are that light, and the feeling of smallness will vanish once and for all."

Change Attitude, Not Lifestyle

Jaya Row

There are many who believe that to turn spiritual you have to change your wardrobe, diet and lifestyle and adopt a sombre and boring pattern. This does not appeal to those who continue in their materialistic ways. A few inspired ones change everything except their thinking! They fail to benefit, get frustrated and give up. Rare is the wise one who focuses only on 'attitude'. And succeeds!

You have a fundamental choice in every situation, at every moment. You can be unhappy and complain. Or you can be happy and cheerful. It has nothing to do with the world or what it presents. You could have the best of things and still be miserable. You may have nothing and yet be deliriously happy. The difference is in your attitude.

In life, everyone is denied a few things. But all of us have been blessed with millions of gifts. If you focus on what you do not have, you will be unhappy. If you choose to focus on the things you have, you are grateful and you develop an irresistible desire to share, contribute, and give. This makes you happy. The most precious things come for free, which you do not even consider! Hence you live life feeling deprived and deficient when, in fact, you could be totally fulfilled and abundant.

An object is red in colour because it reflects red. It gains what it gives and loses the other colours it takes. So shift your focus from 'what can I gain' to 'how can I add value to others' and success will be yours. Besides, all selfish people are unhappy. To the extent you turn unselfish you will be happy.

Do you have conflict with the people you love most? Do you blame the 'other person' for it? Maybe it has to do with your attitude. Do you have expectations of your family members? Do you make demands on your spouse and children? This is not love. It is attachment. Love tainted with selfishness is attachment. You only love yourself. You claim to love because they happen to cater to you in some way. This causes conflict and untold suffering. In the end you lose them. Attachment is the single most important cause for breakdown in relationships. Physically hanging on to spouse and children does not make for meaningful relationships. You need to earn their love and respect. Shift your stance from 'hanging on' to 'letting go' — from binding them to releasing them from your clutches; from focussing on your happiness to enabling their fulfilment. Accept them for what they are, not for what they can do for you.

The world and all that it offers is temporary, fleeting, passing. Understand the transient nature of the world while living in it and you will be happy. Transact with the world, enjoy it, but always remember that it will pass. Give it the right value, not the exaggerated value you have for it now. Begin the search for the permanent. The journey itself becomes thrilling. Then you will experience true happiness irrespective of what you have or do not have. So change your attitude, not lifestyle. Your life will change from drudgery to revelry. It will transform from mediocrity to excellence.

Take a Look at Your Life

Janina Gomes

What we make of life depends on our day-to-day choices. If we are made in the image and likeness of God, our bodies and minds are sacred; they house the Divine Spirit. So we ought not to condemn and accuse ourselves when we are not able to live up to our full potential. Rather, we rejoice in what we have been able to achieve so far, despite setbacks... If we appreciate beauty in ourselves and others, take great care in all we do and say, accept life and move forward — always choosing a direction that will bring in what seems like best results — then we are indeed transforming our lives into sacred spaces. Isn't that what a temple is supposed to be?

Those who choose to make of their lives a penthouse are preoccupied with acquisitions to the exclusion of all else. The attitude is one of self-aggrandisement, and achievements are counted in terms of material possessions.

Today, knowledge and information overload is creating confusion rather than clarity. Most of us allow ourselves to get drowned in an overdose of negativity and then find it hard to extricate ourselves from the cycle of greed. The acquisitive attitude says: What's in it for me? There is complete self-absorption that shuts us off from the rest. When the material alone becomes the focus of life, it spells trouble. For though money, fame and property are necessary to an extent, to allow them to dominate our lives would be tantamount to breeding discontent.

On the other hand, consider for a moment the power of giving. The first positive thing that happens is you start becoming compassionate. By spreading happiness, you find discontent giving way to contentment.

We are challenged to live life as it comes. Our day-to-day experiences are the raw material with which we weave the carpet of our lives. The more intricate the design, the more beautiful it becomes. Our lives add colour and texture to the whole. Whilst we

171

are still at it, the design is still taking shape.

Building a temple involves far greater commitment and involvement than making a penthouse as the benefit would accrue to a far larger circle of being than just you. The sanctity of the temple has a ripple effect — it creates a feeling of oneness and inspires giving rather than taking all the time. Your life begins to take on a new, fuller meaning. Sharing brings far greater happiness than selfish consumption. And the tapestry of life is all the richer for it.

When we look around us we find that there is yet much left to be done. As we learn to link with others on the same wavelength, we find that there is a hidden power that draws us all together. We belong to a much larger circle than we consciously know of and we are fulfilling our destiny by extending the quest of life to others.

When we experience the ambience of a sacred space like the temple or church, we know we are being rafted on to life's mission for the common good. We know now that our future is no longer limited to the material. So give, love and serve others — you are building the everlasting temple of your life, whether from your penthouse, that is now no longer the only focus, or from more modest quarters.

The Monkey that Wouldn't Leave

Sudhamahi Regunathan

 guru told his disciple to meditate on anything, "But do not let the monkey come into your thoughts. Meditate on anything you wish, just not the monkey."

"That's easy," thought the disciple. He sat day and night but all he could think of was the monkey. He closed his eyes and the monkey appeared. Traumatized by the monkey, he came to his guru in the morning and told him that while he tried not to think of the monkey, all he had done the entire time was to think of the monkey!

The guru was not surprised. He knew the power of exclusion. Then why did he suggest the monkey to the disciple?

"In reality one cannot live with just what one wants to live with. To be able to steer your mind away from that which is not desired to that which is desired, is the true art of meditation," the guru pointed out.

Hanuman, too, had arrived at a similar conclusion. He was searching for Sita in Lanka when he walked into Ravana's bedroom. He peered into the faces of each and every woman in his harem. They were all in different states of undress... On coming out, the despondent Hanuman was reflecting that he had still not found Sita, when it occurred to him that he had actually walked into another man's bedroom and taken a close look at his wives. This was ungentlemanly behaviour! It also occurred to him that despite entering the personal space of Ravana's wives and seeing them at close quarters, he felt no lust. So focused was Hanuman on his duty and so deep his devotion to Rama that all else became secondary.

In the Mahabharata, Bhishma tells Yudhishthira the story of a couple, Suvarchala and Svetaketu, who, though living the life of householders, had attained great spiritual heights. Suvarchala asks her husband soon after they get married whether marriage will affect their spiritual pursuits negatively. Svetaketu assuages her fears. "Socially," he said, "there is a tendency for people to follow the example set by leaders in thought and status. And if narrow-mindedness enters religion it will result in the breaking of the social order and establishment of *matsya-nyaya* or law of fish under which the strong will exploit the weak. So there is no contradiction between the life of a householder and spiritual pursuit."

In other words, he says, you cannot wish away circumstances or situations. Later, as the two of them explore word, language, consciousness and so on, Svetaketu says that consciousness is neither male, female nor of neuter gender; it is pure consciousness. That is the essence of human aspirations towards the divine. It is important to remember that it is the soul that binds us all together, and it does not have any gender.

Since gender is not important in the pursuit of spiritual evolution, why is it that some religious orders continue to segregate women from men and also exclude women from some duties, privileges and rituals? Religion promotes compassion, where humanitarian concerns overrule any differentiation of class, caste or gender, where conduct is directed by righteousness. So why do male seekers continue to fear the presence of women, equating it with temptation?

Shiva cursed Kama to formlessness. And now every woman is suspected of arousing Kama! A better approach to centre the mind would be not to deny the rights of a gender but to overcome one's own weakness by focussing on one's duty and goal.

The Five Kinds of Conscience

Shri Shri Anandamurti

iveka or conscience is a special kind of *vichar* or deliberation that is the endeavour to select a particular idea from several ideas. When you finally make your decision it is called *siddhanta* or conclusion. Conscience is defined as a special type of deliberation, broader in connotation than that of *viveka*.

Viveka is where there is a conscious endeavour to decide in favour of *shreya* or benevolence when confronted with the two opposing ideas of *shreya* and *preya* or malevolence. *Viveka* is of five types, and their collective name is *viveka panchak*.

The first type is *nityanitya viveka*, discrimination between permanent and impermanent and an intelligent person discerns these two aspects. The attempt to accept the permanent aspect after due deliberation is called *nityanitya viveka*. It is not dependent on the relative factors of time, space and person, whereas the impermanent is the collectivity of relative factors.

The best way to recognize the impermanent is that if one of the three relative factors is changed it will undergo an immediate transformation. *Nityanitya viveka* enables us to realize the necessity of observing dharma and to understand the fundamental differences between dharma and religion or doctrine. The goal of dharma is the attainment of Brahmn; its base and its movement are Brahmncentred. *Brahmn sadhana*, therefore, is *sadhana* for the attainment of the permanent entity. Through *nityanitya viveka* try to understand what is permanent and what is impermanent. This is an inseparable part of the practice of dharma.

The second type of *viveka panchak* is *dvaitaadvaita viveka*, the capacity to analyse whether the eternal entity is one or more than one and come to a conclusion accordingly. *Dvaita* means dualistic and *advaita* means non-dualistic. For success in spiritual practice both *nityanitya* and *dvaita-advaita viveka* are indispensable.

The third type of conscience is *atmanatma viveka,* self and nonself conscience. Its role is to analyse whether the permanent, non-dualistic Entity is Consciousness or non-consciousness. Everything in this universe is a metamorphosed form of Consciousness. It is only with the help of *atmanatma viveka* that we can move towards universalism and realize that Brahmn is the Eternal Singular Entity, Pure Consciousness.

The fourth type of conscience is *panchakosha viveka*, five layers of existence or mind. With this we can discern separate layers, and find that Consciousness is above all five layers of existence. Spiritual *sadhana* means ideation on one's own consciousness beyond these koshas and not ideation on any of the koshas themselves. *Mahavakya viveka,* the fifth stage of Conscience, follows from the other four.

The first four help a *sadhaka* realize that the Eternal Entity, Brahmn, is One without a second, Consciousness personified, and the knower of the five *koshas. Mahavakya viveka* teaches us that He is not attainable through mere knowledge. To liberate consciousness from the five *koshas,* action and devotion are required. By cultivating the first four types of conscience a person of knowledge may become established in *mahavakya viveka.* The realization comes that knowledge already acquired is not true knowledge because it leads to vanity. Together with selfless service and questioning, complete surrender is also essential. Hence it is said that the five types of conscience attain their consummation through jnana yoga, karma yoga and bhakti yoga. Devotion is the most valuable treasure because it supplies endless vitality.

What We Make of Our Lives

Swami Sukhabodhananda

How to find happiness?

Are you reacting or responding to situations? If you are reacting, then the situation is controlling you, but if you are responding to it then your commitment is guiding you. When someone scolds you and you react, then the situation is controlling you but if you pause and observe your behaviour or question whether you should remain quiet or ignore him or answer him back...then you are bringing your 'presence', your conscious 'presence' to the situation. True responsibility is the ability to respond.

I see my reactions are robotic.What do I do?

The very fact that you are conscious shows that you are not a machine but a conscious being. Draw your energy from this consciousness. At present, you are not anchored in the 'presence' of your consciousness. Your 'I' is in the 'mechanicalness'. Your 'I' should be anchored in your consciousness. Bring this 'presence' in your daily activities of life.

Bring the 'presence' of consciousness in your daily activities. The spiritual work-exercise is to bring consciousness in small activities of life. Be conscious of your reactions and be aware if your feelings have purity or the garbage of negativity. Be conscious of your voice. Is your body relaxed or tense? Are your thoughts compulsive? Can you be inwardly empty, free from the unnecessary thoughts? Find out whether your self-talk guides or distracts you.

Why is my mind always talking?

Our minds are constantly dominating our lives. We are entrapped by our minds and they become our enemies. Mind has a self-talk mechanism. Having compulsive thoughts is a psychological disorder. As we have not raised the level of our consciousness, our mind keeps on chattering.

Do this exercise; just as a tiger waits and watches out for its prey, wait and watch out for thoughts that arise. At this moment shut your eyes and observe the first, second and the third thought in that order. Do it right now.

You will observe that no thoughts arise. When you are alert, thoughts do not arise. In the space of alertness, your 'presence' is more conscious. When our 'presence' has less consciousness, there are more thoughts.

Hence when the mind is constantly talking, it indicates that your level of consciousness has not increased. More thoughts are a symptom of being less conscious. Consciously use your self-talk when required and when not required learn to be inwardly empty.

How do I eliminate negative thoughts in my mind?

Every thought creates a subtle substance. Negative thought creates a hurt body; positive thought creates a bliss body. The bliss body will uplift you while the hurt body will make you a victim of circumstances.

Whenever a negative thought arises, see yourself as a witness and the thought as witnessed by you. You are the subject and the thought is an object. You are an observer and the thought is the observed. Slowly distance yourself from the thought. Observe how dominating your mind is and how compulsive thoughts are being processed. Finally, let there be absence of words. Learn to develop the taste of being without any self-talk.

Why Myths are so Essential

Henryk Skolimowski

ur gods are not independent entities. They do not have a life of their own. They exist and act in the web of our consciousness, our thinking and our myths. Our gods, or divine beings we bow, are created by our consciousness. Our consciousness, in turn, is shaped by attributes and characteristics of our gods.

We are intertwined with our gods to a very large degree — even if we do not call these gods by their traditional religious names. People who worship science and consider physical facts as god-lets are intertwined with their scientific "gods". So are the people who worship Mammon as their main deity and who are obsessed and mesmerized by their fat bank accounts.

We cannot live by bread alone. We need some celestial nourishment to be fully human, and thus spiritual. Hence, we invent myths and "devour" them and are continually nourished by them. Myths are an essential substratum of all religions and all spiritual creeds.

While we are considering this vast panorama, let us not forget the main focus of our discourse, which is the liberated God. And the question is: How do we distinguish gods or divine forces, which are liberating from these, which are not liberating or even constraining? This is not an easy matter.

There is a strange circularity in the whole process. We are not liberated because our gods are not liberated. Our gods are not liberated because we are not liberated. How do we break this flawed circle of unenlightenment? We can do this by simply observing that gods and human beings are on the same journey of liberation. We share the same project of ultimate liberation until the end — until the cosmos realizes its ultimate spiritual potential.

In this journey of Self-realization, the most important two vehicles are freedom and creativity. They work in tandem, in both human beings and gods. The increased creativity helps to increase freedom. And the increased freedom helps to increase creativity. This works among gods, too. A truly free god must be immensely creative. At the same time, this god must be generous to human beings — by helping them to become more creative and free. The cosmic process of liberation is going on regardless of the vicissitudes of organized religions.

Freedom is an attribute of divinity. If beings are constrained in their freedom, they cannot be divine. If gods are restricted in their freedom, they are not sufficiently divine. If traditional religions are restricted in their freedom, and are restricting freedom of others, they are not divine and are not helping cosmic evolution.

The liberated God is the One, which, by extending His freedom and creativity, enlarges the scope and depth of the intelligent universe. At the same time, this God deepens and broadens the human mind so that the mind helps the liberated God to become more liberated and creative. The liberated God needs our help as much as we need His help. Without our consciousness, the liberated God cannot make it. Our liberated consciousness is part of the liberated God.

The Tao of liberated God is this stupendous liturgy and epiphany of light, which helps liberated God, as well as the liberated human, in their quest for ultimate Self-realization.

Undying, Unborn Consciousness

Rajiv Vij

eath is not a subject we often think about or are even comfortable talking about. In fact, a number of contemporary sociologists believe that despite widespread liberalisation of thought in modern times, death is one of the topics where the extent of taboo has actually grown.

What is death? In physics, the law of conservation of energy states that the total amount of energy in a closed or isolated system remains constant over time. What this means is that in such a system, energy cannot be created or destroyed. It can however change forms. We also know from Einstein's theory of relativity that mass and energy are one and the same. Thus, we can infer that in a closed system, the total mass and energy of the system stay unchanged over time.

Given that the universe is a closed system, it is understandable that there is no new energy or mass being created inside it; there's instead a shuffling and metamorphosis of forms that's happening constantly. Take the example of a snowflake, an ice cube, a water droplet and a steam vapour. All these are nothing but different expressions of the same entity. While the underlying essence of each of these forms is water, we attach different labels to each of the forms and in the process, get distracted from connecting with the truth.

This is what explains death. The universe is constantly evolving and, in the process, continues to take different forms — galaxies, stars, planets, animals, plants and humans. All forms arise from the universe and dissolve into it; they are neither born nor die. Death is a concept of the mind and of its identification with the body form.

The butterfly starts with an egg that gets fertilized and hatches into a caterpillar; the caterpillar grows in size, sheds its last skin and in its place grows a tough, flexible shell; and from this shell emerges a fully developed butterfly. In a few days, the butterfly dies and its remains become organic manure for plants; flowers bloom on the plants; a young butterfly feeds on the nectar and pollen from the flowers, turns it into protein and other nutrients, and lays eggs. And the cycle continues.

Through all these forms of egg, caterpillar and butterfly, the only constant is the underlying consciousness. All these forms are impermanent; the only thing eternal is the formless consciousness that just takes different identities from time to time. How else would you describe the transformation of forms in the above example of the egg and the caterpillar? Would you say, the egg died or later, the caterpillar died, even though the egg and the caterpillar physically ceased to be so at some point in time?

It's another matter that with our conditioned beliefs, we tend to identify rather strongly with our physical form — the body, mind and senses. We fail to recognize that the physical form is not solid matter, even though it appears so, but essentially made up of fluid energy — the same energy that runs the universe. This energy is unborn and undying and irrespective of whether we are dead or alive in human form, we remain this consciousness. "We are not human beings having a spiritual experience, but spiritual beings having a human experience."

This awareness guides us to living our life in harmony with nature's evolution. That's what brings us true joy and deep inner peace.

Why We Need Anger & Ego

Raj Kachroo

onflict is disagreement of thoughts. When two conflicting thoughts emerge from the same source and the source is your own mind then the conflict may be called the 'conflict within'. Don't we often say, "My head is saying one thing and my heart, another?" We know that neither head nor heart generates thoughts. Differing thoughts emerge from the same space — the mind space. Though an invisible conflict, it could be more serious than physical conflict.

A mind that battles conflicting thoughts is not peaceful. On the other hand, a mind unperturbed by conflicting thoughts is at peace even when engaged in a conflict in the physical space. The Dalai Lama lives in physical exile; yet he is at peace because his mind does not give in to conflicting thoughts. He is a spiritually settled person.

Some of us are at the bottom of the scale of spiritual evolution, close to ignorance, and others are at the top, close to liberation. The one free of conflict within, the awakened soul, is at the top, at complete peace. He also suffers from toothache and hunger; he feels cold and heat; he has emotions, ego and passion and enjoys an ice-cream. He is not a robot. He has not renounced his worldly duties but is engaged in life.

When the ticket examiner told the young Gandhi that he was not entitled to travel first class, he disagreed. Where did the thought to disagree come from? Was it to satisfy his ego or was it intuitive, originating from Consciousness? With the benefit of hindsight we can say that the thought was intuitive because it did a lot of good. Did Gandhi know at that time that he would be a key player in India's freedom movement? Perhaps not; he protested because his ego was hurt.

In this sense it was good that the young Gandhi had an ego. A scientist who does not feel frustrated can never research. A social activist who feels no anger can never provoke change. An entrepreneur without desire cannot create an empire. Yet we are told that we must detach ourselves from anger, ego and desire, as these are undesirable characteristics.

Perhaps there is no contradiction here but misunderstanding. Anger, ego and desire help us perform worldly functions. They could be positive attributes of a spiritually settled soul but dangerous in an ignorant soul. Who is in control? If a mind is controlled by empirical thoughts that owe their existence to human characteristics of pain, pleasure, anger, ego and desire, then the soul is ignorant. When it is occupied by thoughts that originate from Consciousness (intuitive) and are used to implement intuitive thoughts then the soul is spiritually settled. For spiritually settled people 'empirical' and 'intuitive' thoughts converge and the result is positive.

If engaging in justified conflicts is the purpose of our life then we cannot afford to be robotic. One must get angry and feel frustrated to engage. But how to know at the start of engagement whether the conflict is justified or is driven purely by the desire to satisfy your ego?

Perhaps the answer lies in the *Gita* as it says: "Men of settled understanding" connected with Brahmn or Consciousness cannot but engage in a righteous war; hence the need to focus within. Once settled, the decision to engage or not will be the right one.

Let the Lotus in You Bloom

Sri Chinmoy

he aim of life is to become conscious of the Supreme Reality. The aim of life is to be the conscious expression of the Eternal Being. Life is evolution. Evolution is unfolding from within. Each life is a world in itself. Indeed, each life is a microcosm. Whatever breathes in the vast universe also breathes in each individual life.

Our life has two realities: the outer and the inner. The outer reality tries to fulfil itself by feeding desires and stimulating passions. The inner reality finds fulfilment in the control of passions and the overcoming of desires, in swimming in the vast sea of liberation.

Life is existence. Two things we should do: we should study life most devotedly and live life most divinely. Two things we must have: imagination and inspiration. A life with no imagination is a life of imprisonment. With the wings of imagination, we must try to fly into the Beyond. A life with no inspiration is a life of stagnation. With dynamism of ceaseless inspiration, we shall give new meaning to life and immortalize life.

The aim of life is to realize God. Realization can never come to the individual who is inactive. We have to strive for realization. We have to pay the price for it. There is no alternative.

For God-realization, the first requisite is peace. Peace is based on love: love for humanity, love for all beings and love for God. Peace is also founded on non-attachment. No thirst for gain, no fear of loss, lo! Peace is yours. Peace is also based on renunciation. This renunciation is not the renunciation of worldly possessions but of limitation and ignorance.

When you have that divine peace, realization cannot help but knock at your heart's door. To be more accurate, the lotus of realization will start blooming in your heart, petal by petal. For God-realization, temples, churches and synagogues are not obligatory, and neither scriptures nor sermons are required. What is imperative is meditation. Meditation will make you realize God the Infinite within your soul, heart mind and body.

The aim of life is to live a divine life. We are living in this world. We know that the individual does not live by bread alone. She needs the soul in order to live in the world of God's reality. The soul alone has the capacity to see and feel the known and unknown, the existent and non-existent, the dream of the past, the achievement of the present and the hope of the future.

Let us accept the inner life, the spiritual life. Experience we must welcome, for we can learn nothing without experience. Experience may be either encouraging or discouraging. But it is experience that makes us a real being and it is experience that shows us the true meaning of our very existence.

Let us all be truly spiritual. Let us realize God through our constant communion with Him. We need not have any particular time and place for meditation. We must transcend the necessity of time and space. When we go deep within, we feel that one moment cannot be separated from another, that one place cannot be separated from another. Let us aspire to live in the eternal Now of God's dream and reality. This dream is the dream of ever-surpassing transcendence. This reality is the reality of ever-blossoming revelations.

When the Shoe Does Fit

Osho

ife is fulfilling, but you are not in contact with life. Old contact is lost, new has not been made. You are in a transmission, hence you are so dull, hence life looks so mediocre, sad, boring — even futile. Says Jean-Paul Sartre: Man is a useless passion — futile, impotent passion, unnecessarily making much fuss about life, and there is nothing in it...meaningless is life. The more you become enclosed in yourself, the more life becomes meaningless. Then you are miserable. Then misery has some other pay-offs.

When you are happy you are ordinary, because to be happy is just to be natural. To be miserable is to become extraordinary. Nothing is special in being happy — trees are happy; so are birds, animals and children. What is special — it's the usual thing in existence. Existence is made of the stuff called happiness. Just look! Can't you see these trees, so happy? Birds are singing. Happiness is a very ordinary thing.

To be blissful is to be absolutely ordinary. The self, the ego, does not allow that. That's why people talk so much about their miseries; they become special by doing so. People go on talking about their illness, their headache, their stomach, their this and that. All people are in some way or other hypochondriacs. And if somebody does not believe in your misery, you feel hurt. If somebody sympathizes with you and believes in your misery — even your exaggerated version of it — you feel very happy. This is something stupid, but has to be understood.

A miserable man can have a more concentrated ego than a happy man. A happy man really cannot have ego, because a person becomes happy only when there is no ego. The more egoless you are, the more happy; the more happy, the more egoless. You dissolve into happiness. You cannot exist together with happiness; you exist only when there is misery. In happiness there is dissolution.

Have you ever seen any happy moment; watched it? In happiness, you are not. When you are in love, you are not. If love has ever made its abode in your heart, even for a few moments, you are not. When you see the beautiful sun rising, a silent lake, or a flower, suddenly, you are not. When there is beauty, when there is love, you are not.

Hearing someone, if you feel there is truth, you simply disappear in that moment. You are not, truth is. Whenever there is something of the beyond, you are not; you have to make space for it. You are only when there is misery, when there is a lie, when there is something wrong. You are only when the shoe does not fit.

When the shoe fits perfectly, you are not. Then you forget the feet, you forget the shoe. When there is no headache there is no head. If you want to feel your head, you will need a headache; that is the only way.

To be is to be miserable. To be happy is not to be.

When a person learns to read, difficulties arise; now the self is rising. In villages, people are happy. They are closer to trees and nature than in London or New York. Trees have disappeared; there are only asphalt roads, concrete buildings, all man-made. The farther away you go from nature, the farther you are from happiness.

Worry Creates so Many Problems

Rajinder Singh Ji

man having stomach pain went to his doctor. The doctor asked if he was having trouble in his personal life or at his job. The man explained that he was worried about some incidents that had happened at work with his boss and his co-workers. Was there something the man could do to change what had happened?

"No," responded the man. "But it continues to bother me."

The doctor said, "There is nothing you can do about the past. Close the chapter and move on. You are upsetting yourself and your stomach over something you cannot change."

The doctor prescribed some medicine, and advised him to forget the past to help expedite the cure of his stomachaches. The next patient was a woman with migraine. She explained that she was afraid of making a wrong decision about her future. Sensing that this was causing her headaches, he told her, "If you make a decision that turns out all right, there is nothing to worry about. If you make a decision that turns out wrong, you still have the option to rectify matters. No decision is irreversible. Make a list of your options; make a counter-plan for each option and then act. Analyse the situation, and then act. Then take each step as it comes."

People either worry about a past that they cannot change, or they worry about a future that has not yet happened. Many worry over problems they anticipate or fears that never materialize. Many of our stress-related illnesses are due to problems that we face mentally, psychologically or emotionally. What is certain is that there are always going to be problems.

Murphy's Law says that if anything can go wrong, it will. There does not seem to be anyone who has not experienced problems in life. Every time we solve one problem, a new one springs up. After a while we begin to wonder if there will be a time in life when we can be free of problems.

Nobody said that life was going to be easy or that everything was

189

going to be perfect. The question is, how do we handle our problems? Do we face them as a challenge and try to solve them, or do we fret and worry about them? We compound our problems by worry and fretting because this added stress can make us physically sick.

The pressures of life are so great that they affect us physically and mentally. We find that people undergo anxiety, fear, depression and phobias. Offices of psychiatrists, psychologists and therapists are filled with normal, everyday people who cannot cope with life's struggles.

If our mind is positive and happy, we may feel physically better than when our mind is troubled and anxious. Our mental state can cause stress-related illnesses. Studies have shown that when we are angry or emotionally upset, chemicals released in our body prepare us for "fight or flight".

We need to find some acceptable way to prevent the mental, emotional and physical effects of stress which are making us ill.

Meditation has numerous benefits for our physical and mental well-being. It is safe, effective and does not cost anything. Once we learn how to meditate, we carry within us a ready remedy which we can use at any time and any place.

Know When to Be Silent

LR Sabharwal

he Pandavas went to the Gurukul of Dronacharya for education. All the disciples were hard-working and used to remember their lessons well. Yudhisthir also was a good student but he somehow could not proceed further for several days from one particular lesson. When questioned by the guru, he explained, "I am stuck in the first sentence itself — Satyamvad (speak the truth). Until I inculcate this lesson in my character, in my life, it won't be true learning and I won't be able to proceed to the next lesson."

Truthfulness is the ninth of the 10 attributes of dharma. Normally, speaking the truth is linked with the faculty of speech, to strictly say what one has seen, heard or understood. However, if the objective is noble then circumstances may warrant deliberate deviation from the liberal definition. For example, if a person is struggling against an apparently incurable ailment, words of encouragement and hope strengthening his willpower and thereby increasing his chances of survival would better serve the spirit of truth than heartlessly repeating the medical verdict. Similarly, if there is alienation between two closely related parties or persons, each feeling uncompromisingly righteous, the ends of truth will be better served by acting as a bridge through highlighting even in an exaggerated way the brighter side of both sides and work towards healing rather than widening the gap through plain speaking.

There was a time when open confession of one's faults and demerits was not looked down upon; rather one's innocence and simplicity invited indulgence and forgiveness. But now things are different. Revelation of private secrets has become a matter of ridicule by those who take sadistic pleasure in tarnishing the one who is truthful.

A bride was led to confide in her spouse about her past mistakes and then, instead of promised love and forgiveness, a highly revengeful attitude was adopted thereby making her life a living hell. The right thing is to keep silent about incidents of the past whose revelation is likely to create problems, misery and confusion.

Truthfulness is considered a sign of nobility. A match between word and deed is indeed a virtue and such qualities should be routinely practised in daily activities. However, it is not falsehood to keep quiet about matters of the past the uncovering of which is likely to raise a storm. Very often silence amounts to truthfulness in such circumstances.

Honesty and truthfulness are indeed the basic moral and ethical values to be practised in our lives. We must not indulge in adulteration or profiteering or hoarding, must use correct weights and measures and have clean bookkeeping. But by the same token, it is not at all necessary to play Harishchandra before a thief or a thug, reveal to him details of one's money or valuables and thus facilitate and encourage theft or robbery.

Needless publicity of facts that lead to harmful consequences should be avoided. There are many occasions in life when silence is golden; it saves one from mental pollution and tension.

It is wise to speak less, speak sweet and speak for the good. This is the essence of practical truthfulness. Needless revealing of facts to all and sundry invariably harms the interests of many who tend to become foes. It is noble to adhere to truth, but it should be compatible with upholding of social harmony and order, and personal dignity and peace of mind.